The Psychoanal:
Formation of the No-Body.

Petros Patounas

The School of the Freudian Letter Publications
2014

Art Cover by Antreas Pieris.

A Note on the Publication.

By Bruno de Florence, March 2014.

Generations succeed one another, they do not replace one another, as in an endless chain of clones. They therefore find their own interests and fields of research, and if those interests coincide with those of previous generations, they find their own methodologies and vocabularies. It is a way of killing the Father, while keeping him alive. In that sense, God is both dead and alive.

This is certainly the case with Petros Patounas's The Act, a collection of essays on Freudian-Lacanian psychoanalysis. I would go as far as saying that his writing constitutes an innovation, going well outside of the comfort zone of case notes, itself a notoriously difficult exercise, or clinical remarks. To my knowledge, no one has attempted to write about psychoanalysis in such a raw, energetic and organic way. It is the writing of a One-All-Alone, facing and taking responsibility for his own drives. It results in a poetic shout, more akin to Lautréamont, William Burroughs or Allan Ginsberg in its resounding metaphors than Baudelaire.

Petros Patounas's recurring theme seems to be that of Geometry in Motion. Both analysts and analysands are not in a subject/object relationship, where one would be passive and the other active. Each psychoanalysis session is an act, "orientated until dissolved again", and its essence is to be "what it becomes". Therefore the accent is on the uniqueness of each analysand, symptom, session and analyst. In the current days of the One-Size-Fits-All demanded by Liberal Capitalism, it is a provocative program. Analysis then can perhaps become a remedy for the Alone-All-Together of our gadget worlds. This is achieved by trying not "to master the symptom", but by "letting its letters speak and by listening to them", as a kind of multi-dimensional symphony where each note would re-write itself as soon as it is sounded. There is therefore no beyond of the symptom, no promised land of perfection, no Penelope faithfully waiting for a Ulysses cured of his wandering. This invites each of us to re-consider our positions, as analysts or analysands, and to accept the inherent fluidity of our libido's charges and discharges, its stasis and unsteadiness. This is reflected in Lacan's matheme "S<>a" or "S<>D". Sometimes, there is an adequation between what is looked for and what is found, but it never becomes permanent. The lozenge of the mathème can become a vertical line, indicating a locked state, just as it can be opened. It's just that that opening and closing can neither be controlled nor predicted. Psychoanalysis does not escape this becoming, nor does the analytical session, which literally becomes a "waste of time" for, as the late president Mitterand used to say, you have to give time its own time. Hence Patrounas's invitation to swim in (not through or out of) the waves of desire(s), and to consider analysis as "a fuck on a first date", or perhaps as a date on a first fuck.

—

So, if our fictions are castles in the air and if we are orphans of the libidinal storm, does that make us "All mad"? Sometimes only. For that reason, let's accept that, in the words of Mallarmé, "a throw of dice will never abolish chance", and let's "hear with our eyes" the "letter that dances but cannot sing".

A Psychoanalysis that Breathes.

The enquiry could echo the response It is what it is, yet this is an answer equaling the reply of a God, which psychoanalysis is not, neither is a panacea representing a tyrannical oath promising to cure one's suffering with a special modus operandi- techniques are the weapons of those who cannot understand freedom and responsibility, and with whom philanthropy collects a dreadful meaning· and, within these musical notes of thought, Lacanian Psychoanalysis, any decent psychoanalysis cored on those ethics, in all-purpose, represents the human right to speak up, to form one's own ways of life- and death· from the moment one attempts, or, even worst, to answer that question - What is psychoanalysis - in the formula of one statement for the minds of all, with the confidence of the dictator, one does practise at the very best case scenario a bad psychotherapy- for, psychoanalysis, is something created with each one of the analysands, as much as the analysts who are gratified to lack of memory so to accommodate that novel desire by the subject of the unconscious. Psychoanalysis cannot be but a plasmatic breathing liberty within the geometry of motion, within the process of which, a subject creates the soil for its own idiomatic tongue: that is why it is an enigma, not to be answered but to be formed, which, among other things, paints the beauty and the plurality of human subjectivity· a subject begins by conversing the speech into silence.

Psychoanalysis is a Woman.

Psychoanalysis does not exist- it is not solid· it is oriented until it is dissolved again: as much as the analyst· this orientation is the other side of Lamella: in the beginning there is the deed- one that it is not without speech, a tongue that stutters its letters and hesitates when it encounters its desire, yet igniting the proposition of inflowing into analysis· it is accompanied by the dissatisfaction and questions that do possess their question marks· this is the ingress into analysis, into what has been until that moment without time, not because it has not been calculated but because it was infinite.

Many One could refer to a method, an old one, out of use- yet how can free speech be out of use: it is, when one is somehow dead, or, a mere Master attributing demands to its own echo· Lacanian Psychoanalysis does not refer to a system, neither to magic- perhaps we could, if we think of the authority of words to shape our lives· only in this sense· psychoanalysis is not an application, neither a technique or a secret knowledge applied on a subject's life experience- it is not even about clichés we have been exposed to throughout the decades after Freud's discovery of the Unconscious· and certainly, it is not about being an "instead of."

It is in itself, not what it is, but, what it becomes, and with each analysand the testimony is altered· itself, it is an occurrence through which a subject constructs, or reconstructs in a different fashion, not memories, but the points of location through which subjectivity, that is, no more than being a person, is hearted: one can murmur a different kind of time, one counted with heart beats, and yet again one is to form a question· what makes a heart beat-this is not a riddle towards a biologist, for, when the subject suffering from anorexia enters analysis, what we are ethical into addressing is not the imaginary skeletal body but the obesity in the mirror- from this does the subject in question suffers: that is the geometry of motion of psychoanalysis and its flowing place within civilization.

The Symptom, which is Psychoanalysis.

Discontents- that plural: is a symptom, which makes a subject bear an incomparable weight, in one way or another· unique subjects have unique ways of discontent although the outcome- filtered in the cultural discourse- may appear the same in the violent forms of grouping, turning what ought to be private into something indiscriminate out of context with one's personal experience as if the subject itself were the symptom to a brilliant theory of an illness· in Lacanian orientation each voice is inimitable, and each symptom is a subject, an outcome of the body's exposure to language beyond the general formulations of cause and effect- this is the affect of a cause, which, in time, has shaped the body into a discursive one: in fact, not one but another one.

What is the Oedipus myth, if not the structuring of the question What does it mean to be a human - a question that outshines the illuminations of both biology and cognition- in fact, and, to be defined: it is a different biology: for, biology means the word of life· if it is more apposite, life speaks: how can we breathe life by the letter· although the word analysis relates to destruction, which is, breaking down into the smallest agencies, it is apropos to describe it as creation, a formation, one that Lacan utter as the direction for the formation of analysts as well, not in mass production but as one by one· in this manner each one's symptom exists- beyond the statistical silence of individuality, but one by one, dissimilar.

The only certainty being one's anxieties, manifested through a number of symptoms, only to be categorized into a group of syndromes and such we tend to become: yes, if this is the declaration of a manifesto equal to the ethical guiding principles of a slave· subjects' symptoms are the results of a discourse that has marked the entrance of their bodies within the social discourse, and the rebellion towards the demand of subjection, not subjectivity, is the topology of the indication of the symptom, which is, faithfully to the steps of the act, the instant of the subject's next performance· the entrance into analysis, or, better stated, the crossing towards this path happens not because of the violence of the symptom but because of the symptom's malfunction, or, if it is favored, the subtraction of enjoyment from the indication of agony, with gratification- one it static: panic attacks, anorexia, boredom, repetition of failed relationships and incidents- no, these do not need cognition because it is their cognition that brings about their failure, doomed into a system of mastery between ideal goal and disillusionment.

We have rushed too much, so much that we have forgotten that speech, as much as in the myth of Oedipus, has been the marking and seminal reference to one's destiny, written yes but not ours and certainly not the only form of writing- for, when analysand read they actually sculpt: a novel truth· the hastening towards an ideal led to the loss of a place, not a place to bring to a standstill, but, on the contrary, one from where we choose our departures· when a subject reaches that elastic point of departure, psychoanalysis is, does not become, only a moment- no more, and nothing else, than an Act.

On the April fool's Day: The Beggars of Nothing.

To desire nothing- to get paid and do nothing, the ritual of those who have it all but do not own the signifiers of their bodies· the hysteric knows the game very well, no less than men whose anorexia functions of their bodies of signifiers, and seek to know nothing, not because they are already fed up but because, despite what one may expect, they are crushed by a desire of a feminine nature to whom they offer their truth as sacrifice· these are the beggars of nothing, who complain of those who do not bestow upon them but, they do not even sing to justify what one might provide, for their drive is to get and give nothing- and from them the ferryman of hell is not getting the two obols: and the question is what a beggar of this sort wants to be paid for· he considers the other as a master, one that has and ought to be responsible for the beggar who, by attributing this vigour to the overlord he makes himself a nothing, yet not like the obsessive who turns himself into a metaphor for a toilet- that is- to turn himself into manure, but to a land where the object of the other's desire may have a fertile ground: and the best type of fertilizer is always one's scat.

The beggar of nothing is a thief, stealing aspects of the other, consciously, and attaches them to his identification card since, like with parasites, they need the other elevated and purified of garbage so as to serve as servants to a macrobiotic deity· so, what is the beggar paid for if not for the service he is providing· one is paid for servicing the Jouissance of the master who, behind the giving hand he is offering, there is a smirk of enjoyment for being able to present to the beggar, I pay for you, harridan wench, said the midget to the prostitute, So I can get my enjoyment, and the midget did not mean sex alone, for when the prostitute took the money he seemed to gain height· he had stepped upon the prostitute who, she was paid, truly, not for her concupiscent body but for the epitome of a few inches- the pact with the devil takes the form of the love for one's neighbors· give to the beggar the throne and the sceptre of a king for a day and the kingdom will never confess in the future for the fathom of another tyranny greater than the ruling of that one-day.

One's symptom appears where the question is lacking the mark- this is why Freud, when, not when the answer betrayed him, the mark has been shadowed, had always returned to biology· the symptom, which is the effect of the spoken civilization upon one's body, is only a symptom within a context: that is what one ought to speak about, context, place, for it is useless to speak of the truth that cannot be spoken unless one speaks of its place· this day one ought to articulate a truth, if one could, for unmistakably the viewer of his voice-and I say viewer for the voice's algorithm demands that it is directed to a gaze- would still think he is lying, and that would be the assumption because one dreams of been able to recite a truth- and concerning the pre-mentioned short man, that is a deceitful act also, for he was not lacking height but had the tendency to stand into deep holes- this is what one might mean by being the object of, not of the other, but of another.

The Apeiron as an Object Cause: Orienting the Lion.

And if there is the Nothing, the food of the anorexic phantom flickering the body's shadow by subtracting it from the diaphanous of the flesh, then, can we mutter a thought, as unvoiced as the inveterate sound of an echo, of the *Everything* as an object cause· not in terms of a subject ultimatum of nothing, but, instead, one defying to fire up everything: since the *Apeiron*, the incessant, is actually interminable because it does not have a foundation- this is to think of the core in terms of the sun's crust, where the hole becomes whole.

On the Filioque of the Signifier.

The Woman does not exist because the primal father was deficient of one thing- time- his time was, neither spherical nor linear, but that of the instant, of the trauma- indeed a time of boredom where on the throne one finds only a lazy monarch not knowing what happens to his sovereignty· and by his death he possessed the omnipotence he was not gifted with- a gift from the embracing hand of his offspring· in up to date psychoses, ordinary, a diet psychosis if we want to pursue the fashionable trends of the epoch, the binary of compulsory choices has become the ground, the arena, where the once delusions and illusions, those carrying the mark with the classical or popular etymology of the words, have a place- even those have become skinnier: they have become shadows because the daughter produced by the anaphases moves away from the pollen, that is, so to state with certainty, that there can be a birth without a father, a true example of parthenogenesis· and since there cannot be a poet, due to the pollen using no scepter of manhood, one is to reflect that the Madona's Rose has not been mentioned as a phallus by Dante, but as the rose in which the celestial Word became flesh- one organ separated from the discursive body, not autonomous for it cannot rule: but secluded· this is not a mere replacement or shift between ideal ego and ego ideal, if we have in mind the distinction between hubris and sin, or to think in terms of guilt and shame cultural mores, neither the time for leaders, but of the so called team work- let us hope that there will not be a diet psychoanalysis, in respect to its ethics· for, this is the commencement of the orientation.

Discrepancy, not phantom corpuscle, is to ask if the nature of the vicar's phonemes has changed, that is, in what anomalous manner its warrants have gone beyond the father and, from which minaret, have they recited their

motion, since we deal with what is real, written or inscribed-
then, what literary devices are used and how has the father
been ordinarised through them, is an area of investigation
based on assumptions- ones to provoke further questions·
and if the symbolic has been altered, could we ask if
indeed the ways of foreclosing the real have been altered
as well, in such a way that we are not able to read them: it
could be the result of astigmatism· this is the civilization of
the Everything as a novel object of desire, where the binary
has become the last castle of the father before the
annihilation of subjectivity into the excess· it is not that
ethics subtract their value easily, but the fact that they are
constructed easily at every position like the proverbial
castle in the sand· and then again another question arises,
that of the drive and its destiny· how does the modern
drive, since not biological, function- this is not an argument
that does not follow its path, nowadays, but how does it
follow its path· here is where Nanotechnology is of some
assistance, and the nano-process of anaplasis: the drive
follows its path in this apeiron by establishing a
commencement.

From the The Word has become flesh to the The flesh has
become Word, which is to say from the katabasis towards,
two-words, anabasis of the calligraphic letters of the
signifier, one may argue about the ordinarisation of
psychosis, the use of the body as a megaphone, the
alteration of the nature of what constitutes a modern
signifier, and the variations of the place of the analyst· to
this, as an addition, let us put the Nano-father, distilled into
smaller particles ruling various systems: a teamwork· but
the infamous voice roars that the stutterer reveals that the
Name of the Father is still alive and to be venerated, and
yet, if there is a beyond the father, this destiny, this cold-
blooded trip, could be lighter that the nature of the father,
broken down to its smallest particles: the universe of the
feminine, one not created, one that creates· this is an
example of paralysis of the organs of speech, as the

average medical glossary would describe, a logoplegia, and one may be in need of a Doubtful Thomas, not to function as an representative of substantiation, but to make the first move, accurately, on what he is good at: inquiries, for, that type of cosmogony is in itself a quest-tion, a quest-to- ΩN: in this way the woman is one of, not names, but letters of God- before the signifier, the letter is· it is visionalised from afar, from afar- a synecdoche- from an airplane, this to what one may submit to as the kinematics of the letter, which is not writing but sculpting and it is an experience beyond the gaze, in the area of ophthalmography that accounts the motion of the eye during the reading of the symptom· it is the same dictionary.

This is the trinity as that has been explained by the infamous miracle of saint Spiridon of Cyprus: and the only way to keep the legend alive, that legend that Eric Laurent mentioned to where one ought to search, is to have faith not in the signifier but to the mystery of it, to the mystery of the incarnated logos· this Logos is neither symbolic as Protestants support, neither real as do the Catholics: the accurate believer of the symptom agrees with the orthodox theology stating, We do not know, it is a mystery· it is as much of a mystery as it is the inquiry into what has initiated motion: we do not know and we will never know- this is the act of faith that establishes the belief in the symptom on behalf of the psychotic subject, and what establishes the belief in psychosis on behalf of the analyst: this is the act of the Analytic Holy Communion: if fact, we ought to say the mystery of mysteries that holds our practice's faith to a novel truth, one that is not ours and that enables the analytic place to be an oracle itself, more than anything to the analyst: in that manner one does speak of analytic ethics.

Καὶ εἰς τὸ Σημαίνον τὸ Ἅγιον, τὸ κύριον, τὸ ζωοποιόν, τὸ ἐκ τοῦ Πατρὸς ἐκπορευόμενον.

And in the Holy Signifier, the Lord, the giver of life, from the Father proceeding.

Master Signifiers are not Detected- they Detect.

The detection of master signifiers is illuminated within the acoustic canals of true masters, ones who take pleasure into turning the orientation into a practice serving a dismal university discourse- correctly because they know How to recognize Master Signifiers· if one sits on the chair of desire, that of the analyst, which is the compass of analytic praxis and the topology of the Freudian Cause, then, it is enhanced, to testify that master signifiers are not recognized - they recognize: in fact, they distinguish desire· only when this desire fails one may detect a master signifier.

Psychoanalysis is a Being Silent.

A brief outline of the Schema of Silence: Before the Signifier and the Father, the Letter Am.

$S\omega\ (\infty\ \Gamma)$

$\downarrow$

prosoma $\quad -$ (σ-)homomorphism

$\downarrow$ $\qquad\qquad\qquad\quad$ + т+ Kinesis

$\Sigma(S1) \rightarrow S2+\omega$ $\quad$ (-+a)= 2 Prismas $\qquad$ $\uparrow$ $\quad$ σ-structure (Ov)

+

Discourse of the Analyst = Sα, A Being Silent.

Psychoanalysis is a Being Silent: The Illiterate Letter.

From the flesh one enters the Apeiron· and it is truly one· an Apeiron that, not only includes everything but that nothing is part of it, for, it cannot do without- it is the ω, an end in itself that can only produce, let us say it is about infinite letters, the testicular organs of what could become the company of the phallus· and then silence is elaborated through the prosoma, a body yet to be, never to be, only to be a before to accompany the homomorphism of all structures as if, like a terrible joke to the ear of an analyst, were all the same, or, just two looking alike, forcing one's stupidity to downright that the obsessive in transference will do this or that, or, in the case of the hysteric, that it is about a sexual position, turning accordingly analysis into a mystery not, a mystery that it is not· and from this absolute Apokatastasis, that certainly Origen would have been proud of, if in his brilliance would have perceived this as a Lilliputian example of the prevalence of love, the End in itself, that ω lucking the v as to be an ov, with micro o, not mega o, that is suitable for a God, turns into a system, not structure of master signifiers with which foolish analysts play as if the Other is not a product of knowledge and, truth be told, nothing than, perhaps, a behavioristic approach: where do you stop the sessions, at what clever interventions because one knows the signifiers of this or that subject's experience: certainly something to think about since, to perceive the Other, one does so by zooming out and observing from afar, mixing various sessions, oh, let us say, simply, that one fills a conundrum and intervenes· and from this system the signifiers are produced, accompanied by an ω turning them in all actuality into numbers because the subject supposed to know actually knows that they are rooted with another signifier called the master, one existing because of the mastery of the subject supposed to know· this occurs with or not a subtraction of the object, and one may now speak, if this person in question is in ownership of the, not analytic ear, but of the analytic voice- because that exists as well, of two bodies: since sex is possible only with a signifier, a subject sexes the lexis, if it is not possible to enter sexing the letter: truly it is about an entrance, after the Act.

And then there is the structure, one without a signature, until the qualitative aspect of the drive, that object which is either added or subtracted, not either lost or not, that are diffident logics proceeding from the *invidia*, but subtracted or added deriving from the *silentium*, because those two somas, anymore, are not without language, not without signifiers, even if a subject simple experience their violence· the signature, a structure with a signature, becomes when those components of the columns of the structure gain time and kinesis, that is motion, and it is that which defines meaning: for, it is not that a subject cannot communicate and share the madness by itself, but, that, simply, the time to conclude the meaningful statement is different, a sentence within a lengthy voyage to describe that the chair has different time frame, not the Aristotelian chair, whose logic is explained in three steps- for that is the logic, finally, of a simpleton, merely because the alacrity of the letter's Πάθος is autonomous of the compass-reading skeleton of the signifier· it is the *Abecedarium Stasis*: when desire flows the letters in a chain.

And that prosoma, that, that which in this synecdoche is without a signifier, not even real- resumes its signature as it is a speaking being though spoken because of the death drive: that is why one speaks- speech itself is death, for, desire is submitted as a sacrifice to the altar of poetry: the more it speaks, the more desire is located to the Taygetus of the Spartans for it is a crippled function· from the ω, the end in itself, because it has never started, where topology has not even been perceived as a mere sound, not even in the form of an audible fantasy- let us say not even in the sort of capable of being heard and have the sense of hearing, a function ought to have been marked by Oedipus himself when, as, instead of his eyes he should have removed his ears – which is not reached but constructed, one reacts, a split nanosecond, such is needed for an analysis to conclude, for the tongue subject to have the place of Ousia, which is silentium, a being silent· it is where the end in itself posses and inauguration and where the mega ω becomes a core no more than the shape of micro o· when the letter becomes, not litter- an effortless game to provoke an analyst's deafness to convert Kinesis, which is neither of the Other nor of the signifier, and def-initely not of emotions- but illiterate, then one does deal with the Real not with structure but with the a being silent.

The Speaking Being is a Disorder of Silence.

The voice is the timing of the ethics of the Breath, the only object one cannot negotiate· the ether, the other side of Libido, and the Breath in synchronicity operates as the Ω-ther way to deal with the real- beyond the structure: subjects could testify on this, if they were able to speak of the letter's nano-particles- the Breath is a taste of the Apeiron, and that is what makes it oral: this is not the answer.

Psychoanalysis is Useless.

And its hollowness will persist, humanely, like the distinguished Samaritan, that is, to be a good-for-nothing to the Cause, as long as there are analysts who offer a preliminary session· this divulges the impotence of the practice, since the Cause orients to the real – the psychoanalytic act is a fuck on the first date, not a De f-act-o, as practiced by certain demagogues of the process, as if one knows, as if by finding the causes, or, by explaining why it takes time, or by just talking, or, by unveiling different meanings, which are evil promises within the pages of a well-being enchiridion, yet away from the analytic ethics: this is what is worrying- it is about a good meaning· the f-act that there is a need for a preliminary session, renders that psychoanalysis fails to be a genuine ingredient of the social discourse, a motion of orientation, but, has succeeded to be a part of the therapeutic discourse as it is- that is why it is useless· in view of that, many analysts have their catch phrases ready for that first date, have cleverised their answers and expect, like prophets after f-act, the same monotonous questions before hand, those questions that manifest themselves in the first preliminary session, which is free of charge because it is useless· a first-rate flirt and knowledgeable answers, calmness and a compassionate voice: great stuff, certainly, when one is an eunuch· and what about the Real- a question that does not occur: that is why they do not fuck on the first date.

The Letter that Dances but cannot Sing.

And how desire be acted as such, for it cannot be unless
acted within the beatific timelines on a sol key, on the
ethics of the signifier, if the platform's cause upon which we
put our oath is not attuned to rhythm- enjoyment as much
as desire share the musical ear of an analyst: and if there
is something our voice needs, that is the chorus of the
signifiers as they shift and shape in their acts of
representing the subject within and for one another· for, if
psychoanalysis aims at the truth, and beyond that at the
real where the letter's silence can only sing of the
Asomatos, The No Body, one that will produce an analyst,
it ought to do so by dancing- signifier upon signifier and all
without signified: that is what makes the chain of names of
the father move, when, exactly when they become notes:
when passing from the *Sirenum Scopuli*, one ought to have
the capacity to sing, not only to hear, the Sirens' song, not
as an example of the Le signifiant flottant but as what
makes a signifier flow- the letter that dances· and that
desires silence because Lazarus has never laughed, but
once, after his resurrection and that is why one may draw a
whisper that he was still dead.

The Failed Act

Psychoanalysis fails because there are far more cured subjects than analysts.

Apocalyptic Act: Part 1: From the 'a' Being Silent.

If, in and within the grey, almost black, foundation, which cannot subsist without an end, there is the deed, then meaning and use are derivatives of motion and time· though, one spectacular devil's advocate, paid enough to do his job, may speculate of what sort is the motion contemplated since it is not a motion of biology – but one where the tunes and frequencies of the object, as much as those melodious notes of feminine jouissance, are the kinematics beyond meaning, beyond use- and yet again, it is not a utilization of the jouissance, for it is not permissible to consider what a subject enjoys, not only the social animal that reduces the Other into the other person, without considering that the conception of the Other ensues interpretations between sessions despite the truth that it could happened in the mind of the analyst, but also of that ascetic figure who enjoys like a lady.

And why this tendency with the desert, where one finds God hooked on the quarantine of the solitude of the sand-hills, and wind- and certainly heat· as an act, of faith, and not only, the logopraxia, the only true act one may refer to, is neither an interpretation nor a clarification- no-thing of the sort· it is a hand-made and hands-on intervention upon the topology of a body that provokes the Anaplasis and the direction of the signifier as that is shaping the drive, not the signifying chain itself: and to this, one could create a poetic line upon the thematic verses of desire and its cause: for the Other cannot exist without the object a- that is to consider regarding the diagnosis of psychoses, think of it as an-other Olivet Discourse, especially, given as a gift to that one who had asked if the subject has any issues at work- actually how does the given subject have no issues at work: this is an analyst whose experience has reduced the desire of the analyst into a blossom of inanity.

And when this act becomes a true praxis, one not stirring without dreadfulness, it is the Amoebae Protist that arrives like a dues ex machine, not the advocate but devil himself- I mean the death drive, to the assistance of the analyst, veiling not the m-orality and the breath, but, the phallic significance of what could have made possible a relationship between two bodies, one male and one female- the act cannot be unless asexual, for, it is one where the body is used by desire: this is the pre-mentioned nauseating celestial horror of the ou-topos that is destined to move- as much as the Amoebae· this is the de-carnation of the Word, the subtraction of the letter from the object, ordinarised by kinesis.

A Man-ual of Lacanian Technique.

When it comes in terms of orientation, a reader ought not to pay the dues to a person who has achieved the one thing Lacan was very cautious about, even caustic: that is, a book about a psychoanalytic technique- be that Lacanian· this is the work of a true master who, more than anything else, seeks to control analysis running it thus into a static conception and not an orientation, in such a way that by the scientific way in the steps of the Ego tradition, Lacanian orientation has been exposed as, through the pages of that book, an example to turning masturbation into a science: that is the value of that book- a jouissance not even of the idiot.

Apocalyptic Act: Part 2: Before the Discourse that is to Reveal.

It is a pure experience, a real one- not of, neither within, but around the body of signifiers, or, better uttered, that of the letters which are silent- not unvoiced- yet they are in motion, not that of flesh and bones, where the real phallus is to be understood as a signifier whose signified is the object a- one to which the letters subtract themselves and where jouissance becomes a cause, for, the object is not destined to the acting out but to the act: this is the initiation of the horror deriving from the apocalyptic act- the pervert who, avows, not disavows, becomes the protector of the ethic of the cause because it is a free subject to place its being at the tip of desire· and if this statement needs an example, no better to be, than the life of Saint Mamas- a true signifier to bear- as much as the lion he is in-pictured with: to the movement within the realms, and not the real, of the feminine Apeiron, the subject is accompanied by the death drive· the excess becomes compass.

The Speech of the Stutterer.

Psychoanalysts have an intolerably bad voice- very few of them could have become singers- leave aside been part of a divine gospel choir· the urge would be for one to enroll in a series of music classes so that to be in touch with rhythm, for desire does not allow one to be a stutterer- that as far as the concern is about the subject called psychoanalyst· the stutterer divulges that the father is still breathing and to be venerated- although this breath exudes poison- especially now that he has been apotheosized through his murder and, truth be told, possesses all the women with the daedalic nuisance of a Midas touch· indeed, the stutterer natters of the name of the father fluently- contained by a different time frame, one that only a singing gale would have enough musical schooling, smooth enough, to distinguish, for, the voice is the modulation of the flux of the breath as much as silence is the absence of that modulation, with meaning reached after the motion since the demodulation of the object occurs before the meaning of jouissance· one has only the duty to have a look, if these matters are visible and not auditory, at the process of apophallation exemplified by the brilliance of Limax maximus- which, with a procrustean chirurgic operation, teaches what it takes a subject a few hundred of sessions to recognise if its ears have been cleaned enough by the atmospheric aura smelled from the place of the analyst's desire- if not, yet only to reach a different statistical method, some sort of apophenia but based on signifiers, which analysts like to discuss among themselves having the impression of a cure, instead of magic that they do not, and they should not, appreciate- and here is where the speech of the stutterer sounds melodious to those who do not practice a psychotherapeutic form of analysis: analysts are called for to sing more· it makes it easier when one stutters.

On Lacanian Bastards.

This is for those allocated to the Church of England, which are not English, not even within the appreciative lines of an English ironic metaphor- hopefully they will become and learn something, finally, about the so called English meticulousness, as this, this diligence, is a pungent requirement for those who ought to acquire the scent of the analyst's desire, and would like, if their ethics permit it, to practice within the freedom of the principles implied by Lacanian Psychoanalysis.

There is nothing but despicable wondering when a subject is encountering an analyst serving two organizations with irreconcilable Ethics at their heart- well, it could be something to digest, akin to the food-brand to be mentioned a few lines bellow, if one is thinking in the same way of the professor also to be mentioned latter, who differs to nothing from a bad nutritional protein for the brain, for, as such a book is called, depending from the context and of course from one's appetite. Church of England: it is precisely about service and mastery. How can one say, like the fairly minted professor, who even wrote his stupidities in a book, that, in his practice, he uses sometimes Winnicott and sometimes Lacan, to understand- and this is where he is absolutely wrong- his analysands· if one may attempt to be creative, to generate a moronic figure of speech or an idio-matic expression, one idyllic to explain mild mental dim-witted phenomena of this sort, that would be the McDonalds of Lacanian Psychoanalysis- this person is a Harvard professor, no wonder about the scientific reasoning used· or, what about the other one, and there are many like this person, who considers herself half Lacanian and half Kleinian· where do these halves have a place in an orientation, unless this implies a technique based on absolute knowledge, nothing to strike a chord of psychoanalysis.

Their testimonies are worthy of a simpleton, of this bit outdated formulate, for their words remind one of the internationally renowned village's fool, minus the fact that a fool is legendary for testifying truths· even worst- there are those who separate Lacanian study groups into clinical and cultural ones, because the members of a given group are not psychologists or psychiatrists: from when did the orientation, if these people represent it truly, started having this separation, not less evil than a secretive segregation, or a reticent combat to regain the psychiatric cathedra· it matters little, perhaps it makes no difference in terms of the orientation's desire, if this is an official statement or not- the failure concerns the desire of the analyst· it is also not enough to say that this is not what it was to be meant: let us say it is not John but Johnny, and the attempt should not be that of selling sand to the dessert people.

Lacanian Bastards- what does Rome have to do with Jerusalem- this is a pause because the orientation is static as certain individuals trapped it in a binary· and it does not take an analyst, neither a priest as the proverb states, to understand that there is a trauma· this is about those who still take part in two churches, two ones, with incompatible ideas with one another- how can you be part of an orientation if you speak about what has become a moronic cliché, A subject can have many positions· yes it can, but these are not positions- have you not heard the words saying That you are neither cold, nor hot, and that is why you should be vomited· if Lacanian psychoanalysis is cored on certain ethics, those of desire, then this, does not imply that these ethics are not only present in a scene of twenty or so minutes- the session· the psychoanalytic act does not mean that the analyst becomes a film-star: Apo koinu- it is still used, though rarely, in English.

These are the Lacanians who can only quote Lacan, as if the whole truth of the world is in attendance with these religious scrolls, because they have not read anything else-but, mostly, because they miss the point of Lacan's and Freud's practice: a good question would be, one that is simple, what is it to be a Lacanian analyst· that can be answered through an orientation to the ethics, for, those make the practice laudable of its existence· it is an edifying occurrence to ones' acoustical organs to hear them exchange arguments about the latter and early Lacan, and trade beliefs commendable of the art of Lacanopolis, one to replace Monopolis in this small world: and they can do that because they have place their bodies in the middle, a true barrier to one's desire, so to make that distinction.

Under certain circumstances, these practitioners could have been an entrance to one or to many psychoanalytic dictionaries, perhaps to one of those infamous Oxford ones, under the letter A, following the word apocarpous, which a biologist could have explain very well. It would be a brilliant example: take away the words Other, jouissance etc, and one is to be faced with these analysts' incapacity to speak of their own- they cannot utter a word from a given subject's analysis because they cannot filter it through a Lacanian terminology· it is also doubtful if they understand the mere fact that these terms or notions are not filters to apply to a subject's history, ending with similar end-products and some indistinguishable Others- that could be a further thought: how do we speak of words that are not ours, implied that one is not a thief: certainly an analyst ought not to speak as a viewer, but as an actor, one Pratein, not a Hollywood one.

What is a Lacanian Cause, not a Freudian one· this is the meaning of the epistle to the English church, which is not

English- it is not even a gentile one: a lot is to be learned from the Irish concerning the Cause and Desire.

By the way, just for the smiling face, if one can have the appropriate humour for this occasion, a Bastard Culverin is old-type cannon, less significant from the traditional culverin, firing a lighter shot: it is the cannon of the conservationist: this is the designation of a Lacanian Bastard· this text stops here· for they have no other way to comment on the Letter, other than the signifier.

On Enjoyment and Suffering.

Let us masticate over, once again and more seriously before our teeth's cavities extinguish that ability, the hard kernel of the Death Drive as it is audibly obtainable in the clinic- subjects do not enter analysis because they cannot enjoy: only perverse subjects actually, might, go to analysis because they do suffer· those are the subjects who know how to enjoy: psychoanalysts have lots to ascertain from this novel science- that which a saint is able to practice.

On Counter-Transference and Exorcism.

And when this one, this professor of psychology, a Lacanian, one that God, if he sought to offer a testimony of his omnipotence, must use all of his arts and crafts to orient into a Lacanian analyst, that one who has spoken about counter-transference- to this astute sage it is de rigueur to quote a proverb, not taken from any methodic text, but from a wisdom that has withstood the force of time and most likely has been translated into all the languages of the universe: that English one saying that Only a donkey brays in front of another donkey· it could be something saccharine to tingle one's ear when in the place of the supervisor, that place of asininity of the analyst's analyst, not dealing with the analyst's counter-transference, neither with the desire of the analyst: rather, with the failure of the same desire, because one does understand- the acting out akin to pantomime commands not for an interpretation of the message but of the messenger.

A good companion would be a decent book on exorcism- as it is stated and never heard, a demon will not abandon a subject unless the analyst calls it by its name- in such a way the invoking of Gabriel's hymn settles the amusement with the name of the father.

It is not nomination but a singing- a note pausing the refrain and stops the session at the koriphosis, for, the best way up is the way down, according to Heraclitus, as the analyst's desire has its own destiny as much as the drive does.

But for that precision an analyst ought to have a fine-tune voice and a dose of astigmatism when it comes to the letters, so to perceive their kinesis.

Braying is a first class exercise with one's dummy.

Apocalyptic Act: Part 3: On the Death of the Subject Supposed to Know.

The Subject Supposed to Know has deceased, yet transference is alive· then, it is to version our terminology if we are to declare anything decent with some kilowatts of responsibility for the clinic beyond the father, whose long craved reign a given doubtful Thomas hunts for situating his smallest of his ten fingers upon the rotten blood of the wound, by asking if, is it a clinic beyond the father, or, is it a clinic with a different sort of a father: one is, if the thoughts may peregrinate in time, in the linearity of the signifier, which is erroneous yet settled, provoked to think of Pax Romana, an era which, as much as the changes of it could be argued in chronological terms and not only, one strikes a mind more, that of the reallocation from hubris to sin, which is, among these revolutions, the only one that is not sequential and timed as much as the signifier in the graph of desire: it is free as free association ought to be if the analysts ears do not listen to the Other· there was no word in ancient Greek language having the same connotation as did later on the word Sin, with its reference to guilt and the moving away from the father.

Hubris allegorises the poignant motion beyond one's nature, further from anthropos and closer to a beast that is immortal akin to a prevailing Death drive, towards the gods- that is the perverse structure with an avowal, not a different one but the same, only that the tip of the arrow, that one which smoothers the Bios from Bios in the Heraclitean wisdom allocated to the drive by Lacan, indeed, chooses how to die and not how to live: Φήμη, the spreading of the word of a past tense praxis- no better example for the psychoanalytic act· the condemned in Hades- as the celebrated Sisyphus and Tantalus, with the second borrowing his name to the Gods of the grammar, a name to become a verb, Tantalising, and with motion had occur, that from the name to the action- have been punished to action and reverberation: that was the result of Hubris, where the body had a place, be the pneumatic one or the one of flesh, certainly not condemned to eternal burning for, from another perspective, that would be the work of a very boring and failed sadist.

In Logos of the cosmos, which the addlepated may call a cosmology, there is a stance, a true principle by all means as much at those given by Freud and commented on by Lacan, which could become an aphorism is the days to come, a boisterous cacophony for the fade of the sovereign, anyway, a principle stating that conditions that are observed in the universe confirm that the observer exists and is compatible with the observed conditions· this is called the anthropic principle, where the pere-version acts and becomes an object for a cause beyond the fetish itself, for it is not needed- what about the Other, suitable in these terms for a good psychotherapy, which is visible when the analyst looks at his or her watch· that is a true Other, indeed not apposite for any analyst marvelling the enigma, if psychoanalysis is closer to the magic of words: the field is call, Subjected to A-gnosis, and it schisms with its hatchet new areas for psychoanalytic positioning.

How, now, transference is generated and what is the implication of this position for our interventions in the fields of the feminine?

Apocalyptic Act: Part 4: Psychoanalysis is a Waste of Time.

A Desire that should not be Linear- and· a falling grammar but a prevailing desire- desire circumnavigates when an alpha and an eschaton do not infect with an ominous snore the obiter dictum of the signifier's tonality, and when the object, itself, ID self + no equation of jouissance and the Other or Soma, oxygenates the bloodlines because it has been baptised not in the Name but in the desire's Siloam Pool, a cleansing by which a motion constitutes as it goes, not whilst becoming· and, if it is to mention the word use, in the guidelines of Wittgenstein, not for jouissance but for this It-self, that object, not the I-Object but the autistic I object, that stands beyond time and no time, it is about a use of the object cause- one ought to teach It how to swim, in the immemorial ocean that the Nietzschean encephalous has been able to conceive: this is the oceanic experience, to which idiots that have entitled psychoanalysis as an emotional practice parallax with the oceanic feeling- as if one is to be turned, with the undergoing of psychoanalysis, into a boring lover who thinks that it is romantic to stand as an agalmatic viewer to the world-weariness, of the dyeing sun and the serene aquatic topology.

It is the oceanic experience of archegony- the apician comportment cleared of the father· and, because of this, analysts canister, through the shadowy forest where they can, still, to perceive of the existence of prostitutes, freed from the cursing of time and the ethics of the wellbeing of the Gaze, and hear their whisper: of course, if there is some remaining belief on extraordinary beasts, if psychoanalysis has not been turned so much scientific as science itself- and the whisper is, that, this, is the way for a subject to use the Real, implied this subject is an orphan from a father.

And, thus, the same village's fool will argue that in the graph, which desire is supposed to have its reference points, desire is as linear as the signifier- but that is a dysphoric folly even for a fool to accommodate· there are much more village's fools, in plural as many as the numbers incorporated within the pluralisation of the Names of the Father, yet there is only one village.

This is a statement of concern about desire's topology- a map that tries to contextualise an instance- for, so many analysts get inspired as soon as they have a glimpse at their watch- unquestionably it is desire that produces such an offspring, those shifty eyes and not the presence of the Stymphalian Birds: but it is specifically that presence that pressurizes them towards the assistance of the watch.

It is not a joke- a master's phallus is measured by the centimeters of time.

A merciful patron of the poor in spirit, those who require some of the salt of desire on their stomatal taste buttons, could have excused those who suffer from chronic cystitis- a very good excuse for an analyst to stop the session- not those simpletons who still observe the rituals of Chronus, by, either being faithful to the fifty minutes or to the short session that is not variable but simply short- it is when one, minimally, has to urinate- but that yet again is a way to reduce that salt so much needed for analysis· that is a true scansion able to keep some distance from the two eyes of the transference when the analyst cannot do without Id.

If analysts dare, if there is much of that Ousia that is called the Desire of the Analyst, then the orientation ought to practice a little bit of chronomancy: it is doubtful, for, if there is a phobia the practice suffers from, that is chronophobia- that is why a good number of analysts are dipped into the dedicated opposition of psychology.

Linearity is the motion of the master's time- if the knowledge to which the analysts borrows their voices and silences belongs to the subject, then, this process, and that graph, cannot be read in linearity- unless one is a slave of the signifier.

What the celebrated hourglass chronologises, taking this word as literal as it is possible for one's mind, is, in addition to the evanesced elapsus of time, the prospect, and the agony of the in attendance- that *ParOusia* which escapes one's desire because of the dedication to the Other· Swiss engineers of time could have made a series of psychoanalytic watches that would work akin to the functions of the Elastance- it measures the give-and-take of coincidences, equaling to our practice to the dependent and independent clauses' capacitance- that is how one may dedicate a few minutes of glory to the Parousia of desire.

And just a note- Periaktos, a luminous device used in ancient theatres, delineated by Vitruvius, in De Architectura: it assisted those who did not understand, when a scene and its changes happened- that is a watch for an analyst to obtain· it costs a bit more of one's identifications and certainly a few pieces from the pie of enjoyment, one, anyway, an analyst should have given away.

On the Formula of the Onanistic Discourse, which is Timed.

Free association is a Masturbational Discourse when it is not associated with the Act: a masturbator is an analyst who practices without the Act- a true believer of the Talking Cure: this results, if it is repetitive, as much as the drive to whom they attached no desire of their own and compels analysts to susurrate the same things over and over, to Onania- they have turned lazy and quote other analysts for they cannot speak for themselves· and they become murmurers that bore desire to death: that is their proper function, and no wonder why psychoanalysis has turned into the poor man's point of reference in the countries which these onanists are located, forgetting, more than anything else, that if there is a reference to resistance, then, it is that of the analyst.

If there is this woman, to whom one ought to give the outmost respect, that has practiced Lacanian Psychoanalysis in Tehran, then, there is nothing more for them to say.

Apocalyptic Act: Part 5: On the Act that is Real: The Dancing Analyst.

And with the presence of avowal, when disavowal being at hand yet disavowing the fetish- where the subjects that have been called holy stood as guardians of this position with more success than analysts, the subject's direction cannot be but that of the Cause· beyond those names that are entitled fathers and, which, they have no signifieds- those violent beats- one is to assist in turning them into notes proper to a sol key, for, it is not only the phallus offering a Greek Gift, hope, for the psychotic subject by holding itself from the paternal organ if that itself has been craved at least a milligram from the mother, but the Kinesis: if your subject is cursed to motion then it is a pecunious idea to lucubrate how to drive- one does lower the speed not by the Name alone, but, through the alteration of rhythm and time as well: an anapestic experience with one's body. This is what psychoanalysis can learn by the not didascalic aspect of science that, which, yet, has some faith in truth.

And through the apocalyptic discourse of the beginning of time- when an algorithm of measurement establishes a Beginning, to those subjects that are not obsessive, and it is not because they finish Nothing but that they seek to begin the Everything, that discourse is an act with no actor· it is not a semblance but a Real altering the countenance of desire's equation, meaning that of subtracting the need from demand to get to desire- because the avowal adds the desire to the need and thus the demand becomes Real yet disavowing the tool, though, with which a fetish is to find the ground to be erected at the place of the Pantocrator- one not premeditated with signifiers, one deliberated neither from the secreted time machine on an analyst's wall, or, the frequencies of his body, when this analyst becomes comfortable as soon as the chronometer bypass the death drive of his devastate cupola of an instant, through this Apocalyptic Discourse one is to Act without being an actor away from the subsistence of the iatric of sense· and that of jouissance too.

It is not, not, a synecdoche that is an anacoluthon but a dance as an epoch of an hosanna for the father's names have been dissolved· it is to be practiced as an oratorical paean to be moved by the Hesychia of the A Being Silent – and not based on the Semblance of the Fort Da and the Gaze- to which the idée fixe of a golden calf would have been in its place if the subject nominated as the analyst would have not been liturgical enough, regarding this Parousia branded as desire, to ask for a disunion from the psychoanalysand, because desire is 'a' presence with two starting points coexisting within the audible and not the visual, which is enough to help the analyst in the interpretation game but makes one deaf regarding desire: this is the Agape of the Cause without the paraphernalia of the fetish, avowed and subtracted from its Ousia, resulting to the because there is Parousia.

This would have been another true act, for, in the unadulterated worthlessness of jouissance's material, where a ritually pure desire- that of the object cause desiring by itself- the object, that little one that is manifested within the magnificent motion of the signifiers that, at a momentary look, becomes audible along the Olivet Discourse preparing the tempo for the Apocalyptic Act· and, because of the lacuna, or Lacan, with which this statement has begun, it continuous to move· this is not the Big Other but the Big Letter, the Ω, which differs from that small one, a hint for those who like puzzles, from the length of the breath of one's lungs.

And when the schizophrenic becomes paranoid, implying that an Other is created by an act of Art, an analyst with a left over ingenuity and ethics might acclaim, by that same desire by which this subject is designated to the appropriate Kinesis, to reflect, to ask the Same and not the Other, what happens to the little object cause of desire through this journey of the schizophrenic turning to paranoid, and, if an Other can exist serving its function without an object a· that is why analysts must become versed on how to sing and dance.

Apocalyptic Act: Part 6: On the Silence of the Act.

Whereof one cannot speak, thereof one must be silent- and it does not make much difference if psychoanalysis as a discourse itself, playing with Wittgenstein's statement within the gaps comminated by analysts' mouths, describes from its campanile a subject, to enumerate a utterance for that which cannot be spoken· and, because the corresponding duplicate of a dupe is a dupe, let us originate for the better and for the amenability of the position of he who is an active listener and not free associated, that, whereof one cannot speak, thereof one must act in silence: for, what cannot be said is attended by the silence of the Act, akin to the Gordian knot and the encountering of Alexander with what would not be, not could not be, untied: that which is not solved, it is an act- because the Being Silent is a being acting, the he who holds 'a' destiny in his own hands and fathoms within a realm of accountability annexing the gnosis of what to do with ID, a-far from the silhouette of the God formulated in the sentence He can do all, and close to the skeletal frame of the He does all· that is the Pantocrator to which we own, the Zephyr of ozonation of our practice that is not organic but ergonomic in nature, at least a candle once a year, that object of a Cause not being an It but a Who, and who is not, the Pantocrator, the sustainer of the world, but the sustainer of the Word's flow because he acts· and if the analysand speaks it is because of a praxiology aiming at the freedom of the dwelling where the logos becomes an act: thus, let us formulate an aphonic question worthy to be reverberated in the tympanum of he who thinks that has the knowledge of the king of the dupes: can we still drone that a clinic beyond the father exists: actually- can this clinic beyond the father exist along concepts such as jouissance, Other, fantasy, since those are concepts belonging to the dominion of the Father's Name· that is a potential Act for a Paraclete and not a dupe, to understand that the fantasy does not endure a life within the adventurous Apeiron of femininity: it exists within interpretation, not beyond the orbit of the beyond the Name of the Father.

The Sinthome is to Act.

The Being Silent is a choice of responsibility for the subject through a canon's spiral cylinder commanding silence: the Sinthome is the Act- the identification with the Breath, what a later book, on the Ascesis of the psychoanalyst, shall elaborate, not a goal but a beginning of the topo-logy, where a subject's Logos becomes an oath for a praxis· this is not anepigraphic, as a new epic accompanies the operation, yet, for this to be the case within a practice with some class of optimism towards the orientation, the act could have been assisted by an uncircumcised tongue, a not so fervid Ankyloglossia· for, to anagrammatize silence's commotion, the Speaking Being ought to ensemble an Erg(On), an Acting Being· if not, one remains with anastomosis, an open mouth and no speech or one that presently speaks- and that is how an author should illustrate with letters a departed subject, as much as Hebdomeros describes the plasmatic function of a dream.

Speech is only the parergon to the Act- and this is whispered to the analyst as a competence, a device of his desire.

Apocalyptic Act: Part 7: On the Anxiety of the Death of Time.

And, at the toponarcosis of pathos not been cultivated within the anthropophilic jaws of a system of the Other or jouissance destined to reckon the dire request of an instance, no more than the subtraction of the small 'a' from what one may call chronic, the Achronic anxiety to which the Greeks have been zealous enough in dedicating an unconscionable statue, a piece of art to principle not the sexual or suffering, an agalma beyond, in fact, the binary of those two evils of comedy and tragedy sculptured as such within the breeding of an occasion and the truth bared by angst, not as a before or an after - that is, as a signal of what is to be a Being beyond sexual difference, one which, the (a)somatic function of femininity becoming ether tempting Saint Antony of Egypt· the chronometric ability by which anxiety is placed as a before or an after collapses at the precise moment of the experience, where the Diskobolus, depicted by the hand of Myron on a ptomainic marble, is about to release the discus- not before and neither after, but within the defined juncture of the experience where the end of the drive becomes a start once again, and, yet itself, the occurrence, is neither a cause or an aim: it is a soil where the Cause houses its ethical dimension, 'a' timeless one- and, if with the assistance of the ophthalmological instruments, which are made to misinform the Ousia of an experience beyond the body, one views the soma of the Diskobolus because one is not a spectator of what is Asomatic, where the nature of the calligraphy of the letters becomes a foundation itself- not the names of God but the letters of God shape a ParOusia, that of the Paraclete that by itself it is one of the names: the ptosis of time needs and ear and an infected vision: Oedipus has inflicted the wrong part of his flesh, for, it was his ears that he should have treat for being too deaf about the pyrosis of his desire.

Apocalyptic Act: Part 8: On the Agoge of the Psychoanalysts.

For a mystic the uppermost invention of the Act is Apraxia· for an analyst it is the Apraxia of the word and the instigation of the Act.

And, hence, a good representative of this operation could be the sister of deafness, not silence, but paracusia, which is a good reason for analysts to waste a portion of their saliva: the logos is the encryptation of speech and the presence of the praxis, akin to the process of an ErgOn opposing that name which is Apollyon, as the Ergon is a genesis without a god: one can use the confabulation, the signifier, dipped into the ink-sac of a cephalopodic creature when the subject, the barred subject, becomes a verb and the speaking Being's speech manifests the oath devoted to the act· for that function one may use the phlogiston, because that Being who acts, its Word is no less than fire, an autographic litany sculpting its own lexis letter by letter· the praxis of a true lexicographer: and, if it is for a formation to be in the line of its humane ancestry, the analyst ought to speak to the echo of the civilization's semblance- that is why they are in possession of a voice.

And, this, voice, is to be heard all the way through the Agoge of the subject that familiarizes analysts towards the Been the Words of Sparta: Erg-On, an act which is visible yet it can only be heard· that is what may happen if the analyst passes the threshold functioning as a law, having in his pocket not the object but the ethic· yet that is the work of Avowal, a literal metalinguistic act where the craze of the flesh dressing the fetish, not being there for use, loses its skin and becomes a letter- casus generalis of a position that is the Apraxia of the feminine moving within its place, persistently, along the dystopian hopes of a time to become: and, nevertheless, it is no time but the Parabasis of the drama: for a subject of misery to bear the Real of a joke through a laughter.

The adventure of a language points that the analytic position is neither thesis nor antithesis· in fact it is no position at all, but, a invariable formation, laissez faire, that has to be undertaken as an adventured comedy: it is a practice, an Agoge- unless one is to suffer from dysergia· a desire not supported by an act may be, or not, a result of graphorrhea as far as regarding the letter, and certainly not an aspect of athleticism· and, from this does an analyst ought to keep his hand-lettering washed in the waters of a kind enough pelagic salt, as, it is said, it does cure one's dysbulia regarding language, that language to become a slave at the service of the technician analyst, no more than the Adam's ale in a golden prison.

The threshold mentioned by Lacan, with this later water, cannot be crossed because there is enough fear to oppose the seraphim of language.

A true way, curative for one's blessing, would be to live of, and by, the letter- Apollonius Dyscolus is a clobber to consider, and yet he could not sing· for, psychoanalysis is the parabolic mirror of the Acting Being- that is, that subject, not the Speaking Being, but the one who has spoken: it needs Herculean hands to achieve the labor of overcoming the Thespian Lion- not for the faint hearted who pray with too much kneeling in front of grammar's altar· what is the endeavor of a speaking being and of a speaking process, if not the being who has spoken: a true Lacedaemonian made by the act· and this is a statement with a question mark.

Not a Semblance: On the Formation of the No-Body.

That which cannot be spoken, is an Act· the Olivet Discourse, that lilliputian apocalyptic praxis approbating the Act alfresco from the linear candles of time, those of the before and of the after, makes itself current because Mathew's gospel, to whom Lacan has dedicated a repetition of his name in his seminar on the Act- that is disremembered when it comes to that Real which cannot be said, with whom analysts fail to recollect that it is acted, for, they cannot act upon the knot and turn it into, at least, a Hansel and Grete metaphor of finding a way out- and with which one ought to commiserate that the instrumentality of an evil spell instead of the gospel· that one attributed to Mathew has been directed towards the Hebrews as much as Lacan directed his seminars to the formation of psychoanalysts, been in the position of the aerial transition of a literature one cannot read, not Next to, but Towards, which another evangelist wrote: and the Word, that is not a lexis alone, was towards God but not the Kinesis of the letter which is beyond· the Olivet Discourse occurs at the moment of pathos- an orientation that can depart en route for a two-flowing superintendence as exemplified by the Diskobolus, if an analyst is in possession of an autocratic aegis as much as Caesar contravening the rudimentary canon because he acted on what constitutes that imperative itself· anxiety is produced at that twinkling of the fathom of a breath's illiterate noisomeness, and to which an analyst cannot say for sure that it is the result of truism of the conveyance of a mono alphabetic substitution- a letter representing the letter for another letter: that is the Apraxia of time, where the subjects' chirokinesthesian Acts generate a Being outside of time's parable, even outside from the cave that one sees only the shadows of the

Platonic word, acts, that are moving a worth allied with a Being Silent.

The Sixth Discourse, that which is not a semblance, and it does not have a soma because it is not a visual phenomenon, though a body within an apocalypse, that which is not a semblance and certainly not that of the end of times, present in Mathew· and if there was an analysis of the dream given by Freud, that one where the utterance of a supposititious guilt substantiated in front of a gaze, that dream where the son cries out Father, don't you see I am burning, a pure visual phenomenon worthy of the object called the gaze: what a mistaken proportion of the analysts' desire- it took an analyst, Penny Georgiou, to ask the simplest of the simplest's questions to understand that whole sets of interpretations have been, indeed, along the erroneous belief of time, until she asked What is the desire in that dream· what is the desire there if not the father's silence saying, Son, I wish you would have told me· that is how one tries to notice the voice of desire- thank God a woman managed, this time, to obtain the quality that men are too afraid to enter· and yet there is a threshold when it comes to the act- something to think about when analysts dare to practice knitting· and the opposite of Melancholia, where the body is dropped and the object remains, the apotheosis eventualises not a shadow but the light from which a shadow confisticates its dark skin, when the subject's body becomes the dermatographic exterior of a drum playing along the liturgical motion of the letters of God's name, and their silent letters· and, if analysts could be dare devils seeking to confirm the mathematics of such a statement, then, this equation could be in the outward appearance of Hesychasm minus God- but that is the field of the feminine, beyond jouissance indeed: *The Lectis Thing*.

As said, and yet once again, not Ousia but Parousia· a presence that is a Para, Παρά, a next and towards to, in motion, of something that is lacking the presence of something else, for, at the moment of the discourse that is to reveal, a subject, if this given subject chooses to, becomes a free person though paying a high price for such a freedom, since, the body is taken as an Real Obol, a gift to Charon· it is further that Ousia- this Parousia, a sixth discourse of its own consequences, has no semblance indeed, for the body agrees to the resolve of a desire, a direct approach to the flattening signifiers that have been anesthetizing the legend of the waters near the Tower of Siloam, and thus the Act would fail· paralyzed before they enter the invigorating sputum of the divine salivated aqua: when the metric system based on signifiers and the object, which now desires itself, the subject's body becomes the vehicle of desire· this is a discovery meritorious of the Modulor's responsibility- but this is exactly what distinguishes an analyst belonging to that group one may call great analysts: his humanity, an anthropomorphic system with which, it should be worn as the knot cut and used as a thread, an Ariadne's Thread, a subject counts the letter beats of entreaty when encompassing the feminine· do that with no fear of women as the companion of the one who surprisingly has surpassed castration anxiety but still seeks to scratch his genital organs, without been possible to produce any possible numinous algorithm of music, just to make sure they are still at the same place, is a centaur curvatured and shaped by the plasters of male and female· and when one is about to appraise this geometry that moves, which kinematicians refer to as a Geometry of Motion, and which Lacan has called the Act to elucidate the analysts, one just comes to the realization of the question of how to recite the area covered by a plasma, a word that in Greek also means subject- one created: a beautiful and horrifying signifier syngeneic to plasma could be the Protoplasts, before they acquire the knowledge of the sexual difference: this is the Asomatic function of the analyst, one to produce a Being who has spoken, but now

Acts beyond sexual discrepancy: a truly terrifying beast
whose Logos is an Act.

On the Perversity of the Psychoanalytic Act: The Avowal of the Word.

The Act can only be Perpendicular- a laceration on the derangement of the signifier's circumgyration, for, the analyst is neither a doctor nor a hermit and the orientation itself is terribly not an example of an eremitic tradition- not that the analyst cannot be in the position of the Shaman: what does a shaman do, a question worthy to bedevil one's lips· the Shaman is Beethoven.

The Summum bonum of psychoanalysis is the silence of the Act- that constitutes an end in itself, not a union· it can be, and only, not to become, for it is not horizontal as justice is, but, perpendicular for its Spermatikos Logos, Clemen's act onto the discourse of the Christian apologetics' destiny, encompassing an Act, is Agape, be that for the given subject of freedom· and let another subject be a walking analysand, if this pseudonymous and gossamery being were a fanatic of Aristotle· and, when the watered lips of the analyst vomit the phonemes of the intervention, or, when his prism called body, that mass surrendered like a traitor to a timed desire- God forbid this been a desire- is without a doubt what one may use as an example of the horizontal axioms of the signifier, which is the way of an analyst who is the Pharisee of Pharisees, believing in the letter of the law and on the unity of spacetime: what a great example of psychotherapy, not analysis- certainly not Kantian.

Let us descry a joke, that effete one, which, at the minimum, gave the subject a choice· horizontal is the Either your sins are forgiven, which, no doubt about it, is the way of the scribe, a bad talent for a psychoanalyst to obtain, a true position that Priests within capitalism are more efficient to bare, more accurately than analysts· or, perpendicular, not blowing the letters collapsing the walls of Jericho, but an autocratic guardian of the law, infected by the virus of Anagke bringing the threshold onto the fore and placing the law into question: Rise, take up your bed and walk.

And to the pillar upon which an analyst sets the hands of the act in motion, better practicing that than holding the inkless pen of the scribe, the praxis of a Stoudite who knows what perpendicular is, a Being into existence along the signifier but never its apportionment, onto, exactly onto the horizontal moirai of the signifier of the supposed desire, which cannot be conceived within the prelapsarian lines of the analyst's visual space: the threshold is guarded by a cherubim, a grand protector of language, but, not of the Act, to whom that grammatical law and its cherubim under oath serve as its jailers· the Act is seduced to a romantic prison by the deities of speech and grammar- and to the fear of that guardian angel as well, that winged creature having too much faith in science, a true capitalist by all means.

The Apeiron, the Everything to be desired cannot be read as an Henosis but as a Kenosis- a good reason for one to hunger the Nothing, when, when there is no acting upon the Everything· kenosis, emptying the symbolic of the word and placing one's being under the ethical law of a desire that desires its cause, of that first incarnation that is insubordinate, from the soma that constitutes an Acting Being, an ErgOn, of responsibility, the being who has spoken and who knows what to do with the Real- a core onto which, the Oedipus topology, in fact the Oracle itself, miens the loam of the civilization's symptom entitled by Freud psychoanalysis: a holy baptism truth be told, but not a nomination.

The Analyst is not a hermit, for, desire requires that the analyst's desire speaks elsewhere: it is an issue how to use one's voice· for analysts, and, that they ought to learn 'a' how to do from their analysands, as an analysand is still an analysand after the session: and thus the question is, how does the analyst act on those ethics beyond the session, beyond stillness- beyond that puzzling threshold which is not a door· again, without a question mark, for this is the command of the Act, for the so called Καλόν, that which everything desires· the Acting Ethic is the ethic of psychoanalysis- it is that of motion, not paralysis· it is an ethic of privatizing speech itself so to verse the Kinesis of an Act- the ethic of he who is not lazy, but, for such an action, a Lectis Thing, an Act that is a S-Word, a subject ought to value its signature- no, not its letters but its calligraphy- it is what is fired when the image of God is prohibited to the analyst.

And, again, starting with an and, which is an end in itself, but, let it be, if our vowels are not colourless enough and not colonies of meaning and science alone, and, if they can be the offspring of a production of sounds, to have something of a quixotic token to cover the area of a papyrus about the hymn of love, the Agape, this could be only sang by placing musical notes upon letters- have a good listening to the manner their Dervishing dance fools what is static- Beethoven's deafness has grasped the rhythm· the hymn of the Act of love has to be giggled by the stanzas of the La noche oscura del alma- but in search of the cause's direction: for each subject is different, nevertheless- if there should be just one tyrannical mention of the incarnation of Logos that hosts the signifiers of subjectivity forming the arena of the Act, a law by which the practice is bound aiming at the analyst's tympanum and upon which that cherubim mentioned arms its own S-word not allowing that object causing desire to move, that should have been Mansoor el-Hallaj, the Sufi crucified for claiming identity with God· this is why the Act is essential· because speech alone is death- speech alone is God: a desire in the linearity of God, is Death· desire kills· it kills, because, the Act's initiation marks its own death as soon as the Anagke disappears- the Act is not a semblance.

And if perversion hosts the etymology of the willfully determined or disposed to go counter to what is expected and ordesired, a word which could be written as or-desired, then, the command not belonging to the stones of Moses, that one saying Your sins are forgiven, are the words, the free association of the Pharisees· Take your bed and walk – oh, that is an Act certainly· a vertical act is the perversity of the word of the Pharisee: disavowing the talking cure since the act cures talking and the analyst's infected ears- the vertical Act is a S-word· the Act is an end in itself, if it is the spermatozoon of the ethic and desire that, at the same time, brought it to life and caused its dissolution· the Act is a S-word: the A and the Ω, letters which are not God because the Drive has four components and an ethic.

On the Act Treating the Psychoanalyst.

The analyst does not own a proboscis· free Association is an anathema for the act of treating the psychoanalyst- if analysis itself is the treatment domiciling at the analyst· free association as the despicable for the conduction of an analysis has been the folly of follies of our practise, if, as Lacan said, psychoanalysis is the treatment the analyst reintroduces from an analysand- more than that, it is the treatment analysis aftereffects from being created each time o'er· it substances the analyst into the papal chair of the he who receives the discourse or, equally, he who is a subject supposed to know what goes on with this discursive subject that suffers, when, in fact, it is the catholicon, a blameless portion of an antidote for the subject supposed to know· what is the Act when this entrance occurs in the form of a demand for analysis, if not the demand of a poet, as much as Ovid, to hear the synthetic amalgam of an innovative rhyme, of a Ποίησης that is a creation, which will rediscover and reinvent psychoanalysis once again, a Ποίησης reinventing, truly, two poets, equally, and which it cannot be unless the poets Act- there should be a question mark here.

Not free association but a laisser passer myringotomy so that this subject listens freely- that is how psychoanalysis ought to be practiced: and if the analysand' s engrossing into analysis is a progeny of an Act, what does this disseminates with the trumpet of the king's fool, for the subject in formation, once again, the analyst to be because of this new entrance, if analysis is the encounter not of a subject of free association but of one of free listening- not Energetic but *Energon*, within the Act: it is the praxis of an encounter of an illicit meeting for the breathing spell of economy of one's desire, for it is something of a value, as much as oxygen· and, when the adulterated lungs of a dying dinosaur eloquent the air of an aspiration, one not converted even with a death- because its negotiation would mean another sort of death- the point here is not Lazarus who has never smiled but once- but the ErgOn taking up the place of the disproportionate impecunious sought by the myth of Lamella, as the edifice of the structure is feminized to a Kinesis and plasticity, an elasticity of shear, that of the plasma, to which analysts hiding behind the moronic mask nominated as a position, in this case the position of the analyst, do not know how to Act, to form an ErgOn upon the capitalistic discourse of extortion- too much for the sake of nothing.

A position is defined with what an ideal requires, certain edicts incarnate and made flesh through a parataxis localized on their result, their parabasis or anabasis- an Anabatic wind makes the Act difficult as, those noble analysts, became the superego of the practice of free speech and free praxis for we are experience too many species of new parrots belonging, not so much, in the group of those Psittaciformes· it is sordid to receive those excruciating to the ear exclamations imitating anthropic voices yet hard drums to the pulsation of the tympanic membrane, mimickers talking about positions within civilization· and if this commotion and sophisticated compost of a tree to die are the results of an analysis, the formation of such a boring beings, it is not an extraterrestrial sensation that analysis is not hunted for and fails to launch, not a position, but a notion of orientation within a given inventive culture· each subject is different, has been said, and quite accurately· what, though, would have been a pulchritudinous dedication to be voiced by the practise itself, and those Pharisees to be mentioned and have been mentioned elsewhere, is that, no, not that every subject is different, but, that every analysis is different because analysis is a creation: and from a so called position this cannot ensue· it stalemates those whose desire is not the an instrument of Magellan to a voyage, for their practise, onto the analytic chair: very comfy, indeed, for one to Act- that is why the Act is the cure for boredom and for analysts' haemorrhoids resulting from too much sedentary: no analyst has ever been a sports' legend.

On the Act that Responds to the Real Father.

The Father of the real is an abyssopelagic possession of the subject's being- it could be the exceptional exploit of Lithargoel, a chauffeur of the signifier's flesh epithelium where it battles the angaria of those realizations of the imaginary and symbolic dimensions, and where the question of what is a being, a human being, consists of pure symbolism: and he who manages to achieve that symbolism of a voice that actually appreciates the visual, not a speaking being in this case, is but a servant of cannibalism- let him who has just killed lust the meat of a human being: it is a symbolization of hunger, an example of the antithesis of incarnation, that the gesture of the kinesis verves from the flesh and it becomes word· there is a symbol, yet, one that is real: humanity becomes, truly, something to taste and chew on: that is what an anthropophagous has testified, and we could learn at least a page of bad news regarding the oral object, by ranging an apologized earlobe to his toxic testimony.

The Act hollers, as much as the hunger of that beast who is terrible enough to symbolise everything, the Legion, by its name- unquestionably not an acting out where the message demands for an interpretation, but, it is the messenger itself, which is in plural, that wants not, not to be nominated but forced to give up the matronymic letters and be directed towards the ether of a precipice due to the sorrow of not owning a patronymic body, not any more, for, the Act is the praxis of humanity to which the analyst is the defender of its cause· the malevolent persistence of a Real father is to embody the whole body within the cage of a symbol, not to symphonise it altogether real as it is the happenstance with schizophrenia· not real but a real symbolism- it is then that a mouth becomes anthropophagus and consumes anthropological epidermis, a deprivation incidence of the entire of the signifying canonical mass, that which may be called a physique, now a curious taste for he who has identified with the object veiling the void and its carnivorous attributes: not a fetish because the *apheresis* includes the hologram of the Same.

The Act responding to the Real Father is one violating analysts' velocity- that is why the act cannot be but perpendicular- and, let us use the word hence, hence the analyst accommodating a remedy, what one may fashion as a placid counteractant, if this someone is a maestro of onomatopoeia, from the psychoanalysand to experience a discourse neither as a written text to be read nor as a cenotaphic monument, but as a provenance to evaporate, as a much as a plasma on the backbones of God's body, not a urinary trait but Uranus itself· for, a discourse that is skilled as a memorial, is, indeed, a topographical map, yet one missing the constituent of life as much as that of the beast in need to be driven: the drive, which is not motion but in motion- and in the worst case scenario, if, as analysts and subjects we are disaster-prone when desire misses its anthropic aim to speak of the what is written, and read, placing the discourse on no more than on a document with the ink of an octopus, it is the assemblage of an 'a' unusual subject, an analyst, who thinks it reads and hears what cannot be said without the Act: that is another Real Father to treat with by the notorious precision of a S-word.

The psychoanalyst as much as the psychoanalysand are not discursive formations alone, but of the Act as well· a written phenomenon of the kind of a mirage, be that spoken or unspoken, could be the sophisticated artifact of a system analysis and the verbatim gloomy labour of a good psychotherapist: and yet analysts hum in their case studies about the Other, never on their Act upon the discourse that is in motion- and, the worst kind is he who is not a scribe but an editor- because the medians of the discourse, as they comprehend it, enflames them to probe ill-advised questions, such as, why is this written here and not there, as if, by this, one has a conception of the session's topology: those autopsies are irresponsible, not much need to explain it, because analysts ought to, at least, know about the animation of the poetic license when it comes to the principle and medium of free association and the subject of the unconscious· there could be an Act upon this genus of analysts, those relishing the vehement absurdity of the Real Father: truly, too many analysts to be are resting in their bellies- the real father is most of the time a subject enamelled psychoanalyst: a given for those analysands who dream of hunting some sort of an evil· yes-this is psychoanalysis own, as they say, fear of the Jews.

On the Act that is One.

And when Lacan, apothegmatically, spoke of the drive within the letters of Heraclitus' aphorism, with the Βίος and Βίος, it is a question of a Βίωμα when retorting of the Act from an interval that is not contemporaneous: it is one, for, no Act represents oneself for one another as does the signifier or as does the drive- the act is a metamorphosis, it is not emulating- the Same of the Act can only be a doing, a doing that it can epitomise oneself for one another: the doing is not psychoanalysis or a formation, but it can spark its octosyllabic calisthenics from a locus, that of the analyst who thinks he is not autistic, as much as the signifier's simulacrum, he thinks he overhears words been reiterated within the course of an analysis: that is a doing.

A doing with a meritorious symmetry could be equal to the spectre of Dante's Beatrice, and, as much as the signifiers and the drive are repeated, but not to the Act because the Act is one: the Act is only contemporary and cuddles the object of desire, not in an elliptical or cryptic modus, but, in the unbend approach of the Equator, or of the contrivance of the Deus ex Machina's hand, as it ranges the object, or, the object in motion reaches the Act, if one wants to be ingenuous with the enigma of what sort of an occurrence is a session, which is speaking, yet too difficult for analysts to speak about it- for, they do not Act: but they are do-ing· and, if the subject knows what to do with the real and, having the assumption with the object 'a' as well, then, the act does not miss the object as the drive does· it is in use and service of the cause and of desire, which is elsewhere, not in the realm of the signifier- and a tongue that is hopeless when facing infected metaphors, claims its will with an axe, mesmerizing that this style of statements turn psychoanalysis into a beautiful woman, one not existing:

yes· it is a metamorphosis of another type of a Golden Ass: a beast definitely big-headed.

The strategy is not an Act- it even surpasses the debriefing preliminary of the treatment of psychosis· which, yes, there could have occurred an act with it simply by opening a mouth and asking that big-headed creature one sees in the mirror, a donkey not speaking but braying, if the question prior to the treatment of psychosis should have been pragmatically closer to how does the psychosis treat the analyst· not a strategy but a symptomatic occurrence that happens unexpectedly· it is not a gamble as nothing is at stake, neither loss nor victory: Veni, Vidi, Vici was verbalised for the triumph of surpassing the river, but, again with Heraclitus, we have a testimony that, even if the subject steps in the same place, the waters cannot be the same- that is why the Act cannot represent itself for one another, and only a doing can· if the Act is cored on the stages of, either meaning or existence, it is a doing serving a reductive knowledge to which the analyst serves as a technician and not a subject within, not in, formation· and, as long as the subject of analysis is a psychoanalyst, the questions of Who Acts and From what position, will deserve the answer of pluralisation of the Who, and, the second one, from a motion, never from a so called position- which is the fissure of the pre-mentioned asinine creature- not a metaphorical one since the description was indeed for a donkey.

The Act, which is Alien- Neither of the Other nor the Same.

The determination of the Act is not truth- if it is concomitant to a veracity it converts aphaeretic and not free from the doing, a labour with a parent, when, in itself, is parthenogenesis: the Act does not obligate the father· it is not a doing but an undoing· and, at the momentum of its telescopic sepulchre, a force into space of its iridescent from the desolation of desire, that which sanctions for the principle that is higher than the fundamental decree and makes silence the consecrated substance of the Act, the analyst is backed by the Death drive and horror, the excess that is a confidant when oncoming the feminine and, the only Organon that has the capacity to range that remoteness into the meadow, which is Apeiron, beyond the Other and Same into what is Alien to speech itself.

And, if the practise came to be signified by Freud as psychoanalysis and hysterisised with autonomy from the ideal, by Lacan, enchanting analysts one step earlier to that demesne of the womanly wave, which is accurate to the kernel of scientific reasoning asking the right questions for the inquiry of what does it mean to be a human, starting from the purely not systematic step of the hypothesis and not that of a thesis or antithesis, those positions of the Other or of the Same, the Act is Alien to the discourse supporting the semblance of that knowledge, with which a system is fed its wildflowers, provoking or violating analysts' desire by tempting them to ask So what is an Act, reducing the mystery and magic of psychoanalysis into the tools of a technique, not very different from those simpletons asking How does one recognize masters signifiers· in this case the act, which is Alien, is Alien for them because of those latter questions· it is, even more foreign, to the scribes, the editors, and the grammatical slaves, those linguists and philologists: to those, God's response is that he is too bored with their excessive praising and Ave Marias- the Act cannot be acted by the wankers of imitation because they cannot harvest anything outside mimicry- but they are true actors for their nobility honours the nature of semblance.

And, let us transport motion and distance to the monotonic conversation, just to tease one's underarms to produce some blameless giggling, amusement if we are destined to be called propitious and residence laughter in the vacancy of an impossible metaphor, another sort of an Act that analysts cannot cultivate as they are trapped into the isolating dirt of a self-contained irony· and let us shoulder that this homily is a long-bow, one in the hands of the analysts, whose fingers are not accumulated in bending the string of a long-shot as it is not the proper business of a parrot- when desire is at play, then, indeed, the mountain, akin to the object causing that desire, produces those elongated legs spoken by Nietzsche, and reaches the prophet, because desire moves mountains: that is an Act, when, not the Prophet approaching the mountain but, when, the miraculous Alien, when the mountain drives to the prophet to decompose its omnipotence from laziness and fear· a suitable question for an idiot, who must be a good analyst, functioning from a topology Alien to that of the hypothesis, could be, How does desire move mountains: dear simpleton: just an Open Sesame is enough, only that the retort must acquire the proper musical notes.

The Act is not Alien to the handy man· this subject prays just enough, too little, and Acts much, an ethic not too altered from the Agoge, that of the Spartans, and his being is the Organon of the Act: the philologist is a coward, too much of a politically correct lover that women, as much as

God, get bored easily· the Woman is God- the Woman is Alien· God though is not the Woman unless he is feminized- an existence that exists by been Alien: that is the work of an Act coming like an arrow from afar onto a position, from that long-bow whose intention sphinxlikes the analyst too, because it inactions his bulimia- the bulimia of his ears pickpocketing the ground of the desire· just ask an analyst Who was the father of Zebedee's children- the answer is either of the Other or of the Same, unless it is directed to those analysts who think they are the children of that Name or of Zebedee himself- and, it would have been Alien to the Other or the Same, the Act, if one of those biblical analysts would have attempted to re-action to the demand with the long-bow of a depersonalised grammar, without a name, un-subjected to the letters· and in such a manner the Act executes the command introducing its own death- the sacrifice of the location where one finds the dupe· and there is dupe because there is a subject supposed to know: there is nothing Alien about the latter- there is no psychoanalysis too: that is an exceptionally good reason for subjects in analysis to start praying- when there is no Act.

A Cause to Die for: Psychoanalysis or Death.

Knowing what to do with the Real is a start, not the end, even if this implies a certain end in a subject's analysis- the recognition of desire and the not acting on it because of the cost implied is no different than neurosis for there is, still, the irresponsible being, one that is not silent and keeps talking, absolutely a bigmouth who chews around the same object with which It, this subject, has been producing a diachronic homicide in the direction of its desire· unless an Act, there cannot be desire, one sculpted on a human mass as not an object to die for, but a Cause to die for, that is, how a subject chooses to live towards the body's death- undeniably not an independence clause· and to utilise a bitten tongue by the fangs surrounding its motion so to produce an asthmatic lungful equal to a value, a tongue slavered with insufficient but strenuous words, an unswerving discourse towards those who have chosen the Cause, a message not emphysematous or written by a poison pen, but, one equivalent to an onus, and not anus, ought to cylinder within the auricles of analysts, indeed, because it was their own choice and accountability the service to the Cause, which cannot be but in-human as much as it is in-formation: Psychoanalysis or Death.

It is or it is not- this is the essential Act required on essence itself when enlisting one's being in the facility of a cause: Freud and Lacan have exemplified not paraphernalia for imitation but how analysts could be in formation· what is a death· psychoanalysis letters various miscellanies, with most communal the death of desire and the somatic one· servicing the death drive transpires on the cost of capitulating desire: that is a death, not so much when the subject enjoys its desire too little, but, when it does not Act on it: too much speaking leads to impoverishment, such proverbs have stated and analysts do not seem to discern this· but when the subject capitalises on its desire, an economical act within capitalism, then how does death change its denotation and the face of Charon obtains tint and shadows- for the living death is the subject's expenditure by the signifier in a disproportionate gesticulation regarding desire, when one's being is placed on the antibody of the cause, a germ by nature to which analysts pursue its antibiotics, that Cause which psychoanalysis' own existence, ever since Freud, has been brought to the animatronics of discourse from the hole belonging to the conversational civilisation that is not a tombstone, so as to scratch, out of it, choice, from the permanently sprouting to be excessive death drive: Necrosis- that is the description, and that is an analysis which does not include the real of the ethics- as whispered the real is the Ethics, and it is an Act spawned by analysts' and subjects' being· desire cannot be necrophilic, that is, word by word, love for the dead or death: but it can be necrogenic- born out of death: that is how Freud has conceived psychoanalysis· it is the flair of Charon to humanity.

Psychoanalysis is life and that arrays the acreage for a subject's practicality, not the position but the whole being, which is the *Agoga*, a forced choice that no subject in creation can escape: for, it is a groundswell alighting from the object to die for, onto and within the cause to die for, and the subject in formation as well as the analyst, incarnate, made flesh, which is to say that psychoanalysis reasons for its attendance because of the dealing with the death drive through the formation of analysts via desire.

And by coarsely proclaiming that psychoanalysis is civilisation's prosopopoeia, a factual landscape of encirclement of what fails in a society to be a classic exemplar of the means of self-determination and not of the ferocious instituting of a new ideal, be that with its consequences, a cause of freedom and responsibility, psychoanalysts cannot obtain not even the resemblance of the characterization of the heroic act serving that cause, a result which is death by itself: the thoughts are impenetrable between four walls, however, this is not a good example of a square logic- not even a triangular one· the Death Drive is the object of the practise, so we cannot but be fragment of this unavoidable, for subjects, forced choice of life itself· it is a choice and a responsibility: *Psicoanálisis o Muerte*: that is a statement that psychoanalyst ought to think of.

On the Register of the Act.

The very element of the analytic Act is silence- that, a Being Silent and Eupnoea, which analysts disremember to honour their anamnesis, and whose anamorphosis alongside the act reserves the speaking being, the he-dummy who attempts to say that which cannot be said for the sake of the phallus· it is an ErgOn, the diacritical object of psychoanalysis and the inhabitation of the visceral beast, that animal who has the proneness, because of the phoneme, to become foolish towards biology, and from where the speaking being Acts, been no more a speaking being but an Ergon whose word is a praxis, because he has said so· the threshold, that which is not to be overpassed but crossed, maybe in the erudite style of the Argonauts who allowed the phallus to crush its tail, is that sanctioning or eliminating speech itself- the particular topography of the resisters remaining unexplored because, accurately, analysts do not act in the custom proper to an Acting Being· it is a step further than science and no close to a creed, a monarchy at the pathos of the act where the solution to the substance of how does the Subject supposed to Know deal with the humanity of the session· to that threshold one is to encounter the Ethic, not before crossing it.

And when we encounter the daemon of instigating questions, about the registers' inventory and the Act, which fathoms not a too much beyond the chronicles housing the speaking being, the Borromean Knot, the inquisitiveness of the simpleton, he who does not know but is a true philosophist, asks about the register of the Act: the Kinetic index of the Act: that which is deracination, displacement if it is more preferable to he whose ears can hear only what he was told, within the plasmatic zone sheltered by the motion of the object a, along the surface that is not perimetric and certainly not superficial embraced by the breather of the three registers· it is not *Geworfenheit*, but the act on the destiny itself, an act on the oracle that is in the service of Geworfenheit and the Other· the Lectis Thing is the Act of a man's Word, as they say, upon the Das Ding- upon the unattainable and the binary between reachable and unattainable: the Act is not within a binary: it is a creation to be destroyed, and reappear when the heavens of speech manifest a hovel in allowing the noble hugging of a thunder to mark the gap which is not a hole but a tense incalculable quantity to be cut with a Minoan axe, the Labrys· it was aslo called bipennis, and, with one placid firing, it could embrace both the act and eliminate the actor· with one stone two birds, in this case with the carnassial Act.

And if the celebrated Schreiber's case sought to be a didactic aperture, not less than the mouth from which analysts are veined to eavesdrop to, that one repeating the same instructions as it is not actually caught, and orate of a letter not voiced in a form for a subject to accumulate, then, that subject is a prearranged analyst who has not heard because, and only for that, has too big of an ear and much of a meeker voice, an educational mouth as it was about to be said, that of Schreiber, would instill that the object cause of desire moves· it moves between paranoia and schizophrenia, between bodily phenomena and the big other· it moves, in fact, in its own register, that index pending of the Act: and it conundrums analysts very much, as to say, that, if one pays attention the presence of the big other, this one will testify that this presence is more than this or that, so, they conclude, it is paranoia· their paranoia, if we want to be the latter daemon of investigation, because it is almost funny, to put the function of the big other into the metric system of the more or the less· there is an aspect analysts have never wondered to scrutinize, which is the passage of the Act of the analyst, where the praxis responds to the motion of the object a, with a fond osculation.

Not many analysts are willing to transfer the chassis of their physiques from the so called dwelling of the analyst- that is why they cannot perform an Act, because of the throne· and this is the source of their haemorrhoids: too much sitting on that chair, one invoking the demigods of laziness in support of the analyst who, having lost the desire and grasps knowledge from its horns, without, nonetheless, the herculean hands compulsory for such an undertaking, statically have confidence in a treatment after the subject deciphers or attempts to say that which cannot be said- what a folly, since the analyst knows it cannot be said· and the subject attempts and supported to speak of what cannot be said because the analyst cannot Act· an Act, the psychoanalytic Act, contains an acquaintance but not of this sort· it is not pharisaic- the Actor who is not a clown of a semblance shoulders the knowledge of the act's responsibility, not as far as in relation to its end invention, but the ethics initiating it· and, when the radiance of a sound, a phoneme reaching the frequencies of analysts' anuses to cure that phlebotomized hemorrhage declared earlier, if the subject supposed to know appreciates the implication of the semblance in the way it has been turned into a dogma by Docetism, from the verb *Dokein*, the Act is practised not ex cathedra but upon the agate floor-setting of the question, not a Kantian one, of what separates time and space- because the purpose of a discourse directed to the analyst is the Act· the Act is Homeric in nature and it requires destiny, not time.

On the Threshold that is not a Gate.

The Act bankruptcies the equivalence of the subject and its signifiers- it is Alien to the discourse that is a semblance· what class of an antechamber in the adytum is the analysand's verdict to accept, not to enter, analysis, and to refuse the replication for the sake of a metasis of its jouissance· and who, again, and who, and what genus of a place is the psychoanalytic session, notwithstanding its material coordinates, if not a place where there is no door or a gate- even more to ask is how the session is embodied, as what, in a given analytic culture drowned by the discourses of capitalism and modern science, where, for the very first time, analysts are provoked by the desire that had arrived in Freud's medulla oblongata, forcing him to glimpse curiously a few kilometres further than the localization of what is a body, and to be exemplifiers of that human arche, which is freedom, through the Act, a threshold of itself, by which psychoanalysis is indebted to civilisation, that very one conditioning the walls and gates of their atrophic practises, as much as of their inability to account for their responsibility and the ethos of an Act as, from that chair that imitates Freud and Lacan, they enjoy undertoning about wild analyses and never of responsible acts: it is true what their never thirsty lips shape- but as such speaks only a coward.

The structure indoctrinates the analyst· as much as the gospel of Mathew sought to esteem Jesus's teaching by encompassing signifiers to the prophesies of the Old Testament, so much of the same these analysts have been converted into the temple's scribes- knowing everything and acting too little, certainly not the few and well desired wished by Lacan in his founding Act· indoctrination· and, yet, it confines the Act as a discipline locating the body to a solid position- let aside that the Act is an end in itself· the profession, let us say, suffers from Atherosclerosis, by greatly provided violent doses of consumption of triglyceride and cholesterol: analysts have become obese and stringy- isolated like illnesses on quarantine, with an anemic desire never in place and use· the analyst does not have any control over the Act, for, its threshold is not a space: the doing and the action are under the spells of a position, not the Act, which is an opposition of rebellion from the hands of psychoanalysis' capitalism, against those commandments of more speed and the how, upon which a supposed scientific psychoanalytic reasoning has evolved- what the analyst is control of, when it comes to the act, is the ethos allowing in overcoming a law that is unlawful when confronted with the human, very human, desire- to that, we ought to admit that analysts are better quote-vaporisers than practitioners, for, practitioners of the nature of desire are characterised by their praxis: the voice of the analyst is the Act and not its anaesthesia, a quality equal to lazy sun-stroked donkeys.

What is a threshold- one that has ministered analysts as been the law of the practise, with them not been able to come across it, transversely, not because it was forbidden or marked by some sort of an extraordinary flowing heat like *Pyriphlegethon*, but, for the reason that the junction itself means originality and responsibility, more, even to know what one is talking about- what is it, if not the realm that is not an abode, and where the body is liquefied, and where the death drive, the myth of lamella becoming real, veiling the analysts' somatic organs of jouissance, yet with the sense of bodily jouissance still at place but with no use, with its imprint around the organ than has been the confederate of lamella now assisting this Act· this is exactly the nature of a saint's temptation, however a no-evil if not part of a religious discourse, befalling when the analyst crosses the footpath encountering a very powerful object as sweet as the acoustics of the Sirens' song, a manacle of signifiers having no signified and dignity, though devouring motion and rhythm are moving the body: here is the threshold that is not a gate, where stands psychoanalysis' own death drive- that what we may call excessive speech or excessive listening and it is excessive without the Act, an Act answering to the million said utterance: from where do I start Mr psychoanalyst: from the Act, my dear subject, you have already started- the question ought to be asked by your analyst: from the Act, which is not Alien to the speaking being but to the analyst· the Act is the deed of a creation that itself acts upon the Apeiron· it cannot be acatalectic.

On Deconditioning Auditory Devices.

What does the analyst perceive when inaugurated on the chair of a locus, one necessitating certain talents so to appreciate an organization, and thus not free from its structure- what does the analyst hear when on a Buddha's cathedra, or, even worst, when in the position of the gaze that is apart from the experience, functioning as a Panoptical lidless eye, a true auditorium of a church dedicated to the divinity of the cataleptic signifier, one certainly been Lacanian· let it be that we are repudiated of the words of typifying it as the orientation's ethical dimension· the coordination, as well as the Ethics, leave aside the structure, do not pre-exist before analysis· they do speak of a subsistence, not existence, in the form of an interrogation preliminary to the treatment of psychosis, if the analyst has too much wax of empathetic knowledge for the Other or for jouissance in his ear canals· the formulation, thus, ought to extract another question, that of the how psychosis treats the psychoanalyst- for, if analysis is a question to be formed, then, it is the analyst and psychoanalysis itself that are treated in the session· and, to form the question before the treatment, one, a truly vindictive lord, sides psychoanalysis with the evil perception of a science when, yes, when, in this case and under these circumstances, it should be aside lyricism- a science in hunt for a delicate veracity supported with the subject's experimentations, what we may call life.

And, by asking what has to be asked before the treatment of psychosis, in case psychoanalysts do not famine to foretaste their palatal pores into the symptomatology of the imaginary and the visual, once again, where the mirror of a body's pulmonary cavity is asked to afford the analyst, the he who is to be treated, with the ophthalmic delusion that he will treat a psychosis directing the subject's treatment, more or less a functionality of the signifier, as execrable scientists do, a functionality colorful within the discourse applying the prescription for a better use for the excessive jouissance that defines analysts' interventions, taking the sessions as a whole, because there is a secret alliance with meaning, since the Other is a production of a mass of sessions turned meaningful but not unconscious· that is how the drive is treated, with the meaning-full, such they expound, approximately, and undeniably, and thank God they do not know what they say: not grasping the ParOusia· it was Freud's rebellion to meaningful practices along the thorax of a form, but not human· and, asking what has to be requested afore the analyst's treatment from a psychosis, what has to be treated is the analysts' own language that is not theirs after all, so to be capable to acquire a new one: how does one learn how to speak- if not by stuttering the letters, like the subject who is thought to be postured and crazed by language, and which, at the end, it should be the analyst's own teacher· it shall tell them how to acquire a stupid language: this is a talent of those humanised analysts- there is no worst example of a bad language than when a subject, an analysand, encounters two talking analysts, for, it is there that one could ask what is the purpose of their being, a boring too boring glossoepiglottic unmusicality to be treated, indeed.

And, if analysts still ensure a fingerbreadth of reliance to the independence of humanity and to the personal resolution of a subject, not ex nihilo but ex Apeiron, and if the use of the semblance does not parallax an unpaid water-bill that they honor for donating them mystique identifications and gigantic phalluses not proper for their insignificant underwear, then, the structure is the outcome of a formational process, not a question of preliminary treatment by which, through the diagnosis of this kind, the analyst cannot but be another part of a system of responses to accommodate the object of that supposed structure: that too, is not that feminine: but to walk this road, a road that each one ought to construct, each time anew, analysts requisite to ensure they hear less the certain face of an auditory device entitled modern discipline- because it sets the questions before the experience, from which one forms quite pleasant paradoxes.

On the Desire that is Agape and not Science.

The Act of God is Alien- it is demoniac, as the signifier
engrosses the amateur dramatics of acting in the
discourse, not a word but a true to the end operational
vocation, which is not a doing: it is not the democracy of
the letters, unquestionably not that· the analyst, is not
some genus of a ghostlike being: with a bit of fortune
analysts could have stimulated their thoughts towards the
filthy granules of the been aware of the nature of the
subject supposed to know, which is not, not this time, the
scarecrow of transference- since it unbraids the podium's
stance upon where the speaking being will interweave the
outward appearance of its act· this is what could have
make this creature called psychoanalyst an extraordinary
mortal, because it Acts on its word and not biology: not a
usual quality of analysts, and, there could be a peculiar
something to spice those minds, with a prescribed amount
of high-quality affluence and excellent omens, are not to be
characterised, as Adler wrote, idiots from birth· and whilst
the crux of the moment is at its timeless soil and the
subject's inadvertencies cough up the letter, because it
perseveres, not without stubbornness, the signifier's
latitude, the Act condescends to the signifier its real value
and makes audible the speaking being manifested within
the course of an analysis, something of a fresh principal
capital for the new mounting economy, becoming the
Archangel's ambrosial scale of what is a worth according to
the given desire of the Acting Being: for, a word to have a
price, a simmering somewhat of one's own manure
becoming a fertilizer, in or out a compost for he that is able
to Act, the subject no longer per-verses its word by not
acting· the code of Bushido, a good game of words for
those philologists to transmit to the pre-mentioned manure,
the heroic code, exists along a perverse discourse, only
that the hero dedicates his being into, not to, but into, an

act serving a cause: that is not the act of science, but of Agape.

And, if the amphibole letters of a music's kind enough marginalia, mumble its notes within the session, at the length of the polluted waters of the archipelago of forming a line and not a triangle, to which analysts could have applied the Pythagorean theorem with the infamous hypotenuse equaling to an addition and an elevation to the second power, a mere application of a formula not equaling an Act, because of the missing anabiosis of desire, for, if the signifier is characterized by a certain polysemousness, the Act is one because it is the work of the analyst's love for the cause and not science· not to love the analysand, and that is, despite appearances, the exact humanistic nature of psychoanalysis· the Act is the adaptation of the actor's being to a discipline, a discipline higher that the rule defining a practise or an idea.

The Act is consubstantial to Agape, and, to this human principle of laughter the psychoanalyst forms the motion of his desire, that which Freud enabled quality aspect of the drive: for, a formation is the anagoge of desire in place of a theory of forms· it is not force or brutality for the reason that those are atomic substances of another arrangement spoken as knowledge, which the act is Alien to.

There is no pre-existing register for the Act, but the desire forms such a register within registers- and it uses the object of the cause by which it has received the birthright to dissect one that is beyond the registers: the shaman knows about this, as much as that which is Alien to that which is proper of a space of a scientific function: the joker too knows that as well, since, the shared laughter is a product of a limited meaning- where the metaphor fails, there is laughter· it is even better· the Act that is Alien ought to be outside from what is hegemonic and certainly not near to the bad anecdote of what is science: science is the epistemological discourse that prohibits a subject to reflect otherwise and it is not feminine- to this legitimizing tyranny the desire of the Act is Alien· and, because of its autonomy, a function of freedom and formation, it is a praxis carried out on psychoanalysis itself: the suicide of the Phoenix of language and the penetration of the Weltanschauung of words through the threshold settled by Lacan· and, if science became a God's discourse to be venerated, an absolute Voice if one sought to think of it as a faultless discourse, then, the Act that cannot be without desire, which is of the a Being Silent, is the Real of the Voice: and only through that real analysts could have had some worthy history to pronounce- or else, they should stay behind soundless in their apraxia, the anergy, that position deficient of the Ergon yet bursting of glossematics with no desire or humanism: desire is not Allien to the Act· desire it is the autogram of that letter which inscribes itself.

On the Diaeresis of the Letter and Desire.

The Psychoanalyst analyses the analysand· what a folly for our orientation, and a good reason for one's underarms to be in the service of transudation: it is the analysand who perlustrates the analyst- that is how desire occupies a body that is not victim to the diaphoresis of the master and is able to breathe in and out an incantation, for, the plus one does not generate a law but, himself, is generated by that desire performing instead of a law· otherwise, how to speak of that which cannot be said, because it is not written, if not by sculpting the stage-whisperer's idea, without rhyme or reason, murmuring that which cannot be said is an Act.

The Act raises its acuminous exactitude onto the moving geometry of the plasma, which the death drive's fairy tale knows back to front, and, from which we could learn at least an molecule of truth, from the letter to speech: this is what happens when the analyst is subtracted from language and the signifier- and, if analysts would like to have a portion of decency and respect, so as to acknowledge the specter of the subject supposed to know, then a candle ought to be dedicated to a shrine, from analysts to their analysands for portioning such a, beyond doubt, Freudian cause.

The letter refuses the language· it is no litter- language is the rejectamenta of the letter, because, it, the letter, is not written but sculpted upon that discourse been neither a law nor a body· fingerspelling, consequently, is a good audible assistance for deaf analysts, when they hear the law and not desire, omitting thus those ligatures which cannot be read- it is to those earless invertebrates that the Act offers the gift of Diaeresis, a Parousia Alien to language, unless as a paralogy, Παρά το Λόγο, not instead of but by the length of: at the failure of the word, the Act exists- but not without the letter.

On the Desire of the Gentile.

If psychoanalysis' Ousia residues in the interior and the con-text of the session, is not an Act but an old fashioned Pavlovian usance of a different time scale, longer indeed, awaiting the subject's analyst to be satisfied with how this given analysand deals with his Daimonion, the Other, a function that analysts have revolved- just hear them chatting about it- into an imperceptible other person, reducing its function into an embarrassed cognition supposedly not implied to the analysand: but the voice who is unvoiced it is even more horrible· an unpardonable glimpse and an appraisal without the support of any optical devises, into a number of case studies, depicts the truth, that is, very few analysts canister to speak their own language, remaining thus attentive and attached to a Name of the Father, practicing a psychotherapy, one not been able however to treat their individual symptom, which is cloning: there is no dupe but duple, and, Pavlov, and certainly the supposedly free enterprise oxygenating demands for professionalism, would have been proud of such an exegesis· a professional process not at all human, not even analysis, but the hopeless fetish of he who is parsimonious, if we add desire and ethics into this orgy of professionalism: a franchise within capitalism· as one could smell the phallic redolence of a disintegrating question, which is inhuman as much as it is human, analysis being and present to civilization, to the civilization hosting its free ethical practice allowing subjects to be in formation and not subjected to any theory of forms, is psychoanalysis own Act onto the excess of the discourses asphyxiating the desire of that civilization's subjects- in this manner the in-formation differs from the semblance's information leading to cloning and not at all to the creation of a new alphabet, through which analysts cannot plagiarize the responsibility of learning each time anew- and this is the same reason that an analyst is not a position but a Kinesis: yet, he who is obese and refuses to be fed by desire, certainly, cannot move and prefers the position- that of been a cleric of the Other.

The functioning of desire is naked bare by the mode analysts testify, orally or written, of the analysands' syllabary, not by the elements they murmur about psychoanalysis's pictograph, inserting the Real of an experience underneath labeling and malodorous arms of a theory because these analysts cannot have a word for themselves- it is only clear that there is an Ousia asyndeton to desire, and thus it is not an Ousia· and, if the Act endured in the sessions does not lengthen its hands towards the discourses, oh, those of the civil too precisely because psychoanalysis is not an autistic position but a motion, becoming the voice and host of a true anthropology, that is, of a different reverberation mouthing what an *Anthropos* is, and, instead, remains atrophic to a group of intellectualistic rituals, just something for analysts to chat about among colleagues, then the subject is literally a speaking being- a mass of meat speaking· in this way one may describe a Muppet: you are a Muppet· a Muppet of the Other· there cannot be, not even one, indicia of an orientation if analysts gathered not beyond but along the Name of the Father, since, truth be told, for the ears of a mysterious someone who has the honesty to benefit from an authentic comedy and is not caught up in psychoanalysis own dramatic discourse, or, better to write, of psychoanalysts' dramatic discourses, the comedian's most famous Act is a doing when it is repeated- it is the work of the semblance: it turns psychoanalysis into a joke- and that is meant without laughter.

The Act's is that which is carried in the pavements- the Act is a she and it is learned through the discipline of harlotry: each time analysts ought to ask themselves, not whom do you want me to be, but what is desire· this will answer the binary enigma of professionalism versus human practice- a step to debar Oedipus' signifier itself, if we would be curious enough, brave and responsible, to enter that feminine· this is the desire of the Gentile- the third Act.

The Real is not the Impossible- the Real is the Ethic.

What is impossible to bear is the Ethic of desire, too much of an oral object for a technician's stomach· the misrepresentation of formalization, one limited to a small area by the gonioscopy of mastery, has been proved possible, as the ethic of desire is impossible because analysts squander their tongue's propositions in uttering a premise for its sake and not its essence, talking about after all a curing science: there are diminutive amounts of orientating new analysts but too much cure, and analysts have become the extraordinary coincidence of a circus' arena within associations or schools· that failure, certainly, does not cease to not write itself, and baring that Real does not desiderate a body but an ethical motion, not a position, for one's desire· simply that· for whom, then, is the real impossible to bear, if not for the analysts or a given school, for as long as analysts converse of the sessions within the structure of a formalization, not being able to learn anew an alphabet speaking for themselves, then, surely the letter does not have its baring and possesses the gloomy ambiance of a ceiling, forbidden to escape, lynching above desire like the sword of Damocles· and, since there are, even to this year, questions of the symptom's measurement and separation, as been clinical or not, we could pull our eyelids and sponge down our hands before saying that it is the analyst who is clinical or not, when he is uncoordinated from the culture and sheltered into the fantasy of psychiatry's throne: bearing a desire does not require one's body- it is braying that depends upon a body: and that is the zetetic.

And, about the presentation of cases by those deacons of misery specialized in the thanatosis of the wish, let us simply say that analysts ought to necessitate in discovering how to enlighten stories not from paper, not too dreary for the ears and optimistically to tease enough one's enthusiasm- stories that are not theirs, but it is such a difficult task when one trades the ethics of the cause: and if there is a further utterance, a feeble one tyrannizing this generation's minds and makes psychoanalysis an amount of sordid hors d'oeuvre, this is the structure of the impossible to bear and the impossible of the practice of psychoanalysis: psychoanalysis, my dear friend, is not practiced but lived- for when at that point where a subject diagnoses its desire is not only for utilizing it only within the sessions as if it is some breed of an abracadabra· and if we are in love with using the word clinic, with or without the ostentatious vocabulary commendable of a baroque epoch, and exonerations that we do not fundamentally trust, then, the clinic is that of the letter and desire, and, for that we ought to know at least a word to say about: about the Ethic repressed· an experimentation praiseworthy of a commendable amusement would be to illegitimate analysts' reading from papers with reference to their experiences in the sessions, but, instead, let them perorate and free associate- and the thaumaturgic statement of the impossible to say will glare itself in front of the spectators' Achilles heel, to allow that free association: it is impossible to say because analysts cannot Act, stuttering their desire, for, that which cannot be said is an Act· one ought to think, however, what is not allowing them to speak- and that, according to Freud, is for the love of the parent.

Silence in this case is not the speech of the Act, the doing of desire- speech here is the trauma: what is unfeasible to bear and said is desire, which is not lazy· and, if there is an impossibility in psychoanalysis, this is nothing else than the forgotten desire by a school, an orientation and analysts themselves· let us produce convinced low-tuned whispering reverberations, like old men, about case presentations and catechize by testing the waters, what can we take notice of from the apostles and the infamous *Acta Apostolorum*, stated under oath in a confident manner, which is a good pass and a testimony: when one's being is dedicated to desire· and, a thunderous signifying chain, whose signifieds emphasize meaning through questions, about the subject whom the orientation could describe as been under the anathema of the impossible to say, impracticable to speak, that is the assemblage of analysts in a congress, who, not been daring enough to heave their voices they prefer reading from a piece of paper- what a somniferous attitude towards the Cause, too many bores opiate desire- those, those who are not able to speak, those who are bounded with an eternal commemorative moment of silence, and who are not the same from the impossible to say of the analysand: and many, misologysts of desire, under the vow of a true silence, because of the fear of losing the love of the Other, ought to think that at least monks' silence is accompanied by a practice and an Act, much different, yet again, form this class of an Omertà.

Das ist nicht nur nicht richtig, es ist nicht einmal falsch- this is what symphonizes psychoanalysis as been a pseudoscience: when the analysts' speech is not oriented by desire· it would be an invocation accompanied by a flight of the imagination, if those misologysts have been at least a bit Laconian and less Lacanian, to talk little but precisely· there is also something else to echo one's thoughts on, to become skilled at the exchange of phonemes, and make our pitiful common sense to amend the questions orienting the practise- that, Spartan students were biting their thumps to castigate themselves because they rambled too much their responses· the trauma of lalangue is present in analysts' inability to speak without preparation in front of an audience- they are not responsible for their words and that is the Sinthome of a bad approach to speech itself: it is unquestionably clinical my dear friend· get them to speak, to free associate without quotes or texts and see if they can bear the responsibility of their word- then, truly, then the impossibility of the Real, the ethics of desire, will be vivid, too vivid to engross in the symbolic.

The Organon of Desire: Neither a Phallus nor a Penis.

The eunuch does not put perpendicular a penis and, without fail, not a phallus- this is to opine, if meaning and the symbolization of an apologue could be the intergradient of a sustenance, which is not at the end, when it comes about to interpret a dream, that the devout follower of a queen, who, when exposed to femininity, does not obtain any anxiety, or so ever, regarding the symbolic castration· he, that he without the phallus, does retrospect the donation of the tongues, so much as to speak to a woman's body· the instrumentality of the transference is not that of the subject suppose to know- that is not enough for faith- one does need the miracle of speaking many tongues, in fact many letters, not confusion equal to Babelism to whom the gentiles would refer as bar-bar-ism, and had the authority to recite the letter of the signifier's bar, but, the Apeiron of that great discourse that a woman's drive is not able to grasp, because of the continuum expressed though the Other and becomes the acrolectal optic disabling the analyst to learn a new correspondence- this is not, honestly, enough to explain the drive's anaplasia· the distinction between psychoanalyst and psychoanalysand is abolished by the Act- *Dixitque Deus: Fiat lux. Et facta est lux*- that is a Act, when one's word is an act by itself· a parallel to the shield of Achilles' depiction, if we request to speak about that feminine drive, that which can only be a death spirit equal to the Keres, for, it is an excess of itself resisting the psychostasia of the structure determined by the signifiers and the optical field of the gaze.

And, with that Organon, which is in plural, and which an orientation ought to serve by not producing the sperm of a peculiar semblance, desire accompanies the Acts of the psychoanalysts: the acts of the school that is the formation of analysts· in case a new era Eusebius would have written a psychoanalytic history, it could have been categorized among, once again but not for a church, among the homologoumena- those books that subjects shall not doubt· this is a testimony for the Ethics of the Act, and psychoanalysis itself, which, as it has been argued and with too much error, that they are deontological: that is the trap of the gaze, my dear, for deontology is just the other end of the same equation and, with this application of an ethical formula, placing emphasis at the beginning or at the end, to the Act or to psychoanalysis itself, the ethic of desire becomes the mirror of a binary, not psychoanalytic at all: for, with Organon, one may zoom-in the structure, from the signifier to the letter, a perpendicular Kinesis that is auditory, and if this brave analyst can say, one day, something about this Act, then his spoken letter would turn out as a myth.

On the Anonymity of Psychoanalysis.

The object that acts: you ought to jaw a few letters alleging that the duty for that motion belongs to your desire, even though, God forbid, such a desire is trapped between a xiphoid view of the Other and a master interpreter suffering from otitis: you ought to say, that the duty reliable of that desire guides you, the analyst, to be directed in the treatment and not to direct: you ought to declare, because of that desire, that the Act is anonymous, and the more anonymous it is, the more feminine is transmogrified, and that, there are not only two acts as a technician of psychoanalysis will conclude· there is at least another one-besides the act of the analyst and the analysand: there is, intend this plural as an 'is,' the Acts of psychoanalysis itself· and those are not alone.

And, yet again, the church of the Ephesians has reached a binary, which is not a problem, unless those faithful unbelievers, who waste their faith and desire to the process of questioning, once again, the works and the faith- by asking if, is it faith or work that saves, when, what is Real, is that it is an Act of faith that is saved after all, making free will the duty of desire, which is not deontological because it is outside of time and its two children, that of the beginning and the end· and, if we sought to cough a short memorandum and draw a portrait with one's sweat, which we could surname as experience of a desire, and say that something is castrated, then we ought to glimpse not to firmament but to the praxis of the entity that is not a flesh, but an Organon using the analyst, for, both analyst and analysand are bounded by that Oracle- that which desires: that which wills freely.

The Act is the Kenosis of the word of the father, of that which binds Prometheus as a signifier of light upon that body that is not a soma: this is the third act, for those who love bullet-points and numbering, that of the Logos upon which, not only the analysts and analysands are geometrically surmounted by, by it, but the Act itself, even though it overcomes that fundamental rule defining its practice and gentle commandments · for, with the names of the fathers comes the Ethics of the Fathers, that *Pirke Avoth* of the Hebrews, certainly not the gentile ethics, and based on the tips of a process of wisdom that one may call proverbs, preparing the ground for that Kenotic body, not a xeric matter to be saved by the acts or faith, but the principle arguing: that he who has been emptied by the names of fathers is not relinquished but relanguaged the signifier's divine attributes so as to experience a human tongue, an anthropoglot agony unless oriented by a desire, the new dermatoglyphics of the ErgOn, that being who has spoken and now acts: for, psychoanalysis is not action oriented as it does not put faith on the doing- it is Act oriented: and for that, one's word must be a signature· that is how desire functions.

And: psychoanalysis, the act even more, cannot be defined from the episcopacy of deontological ethics, as they do not pre-exist so to think the right action, which can be right or wrong only within a context of time, neither do they belong to a linearity of moments in time necessary for stating and defining the true action: the metaphor from the letter can only be a revolution· desire is indeed xenoglossy- it is the Letter of the Alien, not of the Other from where the subject is the affect of the signifiers' possessive diabolism· desire is definitely not ensuing from Erythropoiesis- but by the lungful of air of that soma that cannot be a body: not the organism· the signifier is a cacology to the astronautics of the letter· psychoanalysis is anonymous- that is why the metaphor from the letter can only be a revolution.

The Duty of Psychoanalysis.

A duty is not a dept· the duty of psychoanalysis is its commitment to the ethic responsible for providing the practice itself a space within the discourses of civilization- it is the duty towards the symptom's bronchophony in the direction of that serpentine desire pushing for recognition· there cannot be psychoanalysis without civilization, and there cannot be a civilisation without psychoanalysis: more than anything, the analyst is Kinesis, and he precipitates, outside of time, those interventions upon the Letter so that free speech is lawfully recognized: a speech that is perpendicular- nothing more· that motion, not the subject in progress, or in process, is not locked within sessions, neither within the repetitive sounds captured by a wall's ear- as they say- or behind soundproof doors where one's hieroglyphic echo is not only not becoming epigraphic, but, it is swallowed by the catatonia of the analyst's own desire· when analysts speak their voices ought to crumble the walls of Jericho, of that Ιερός Ήχος of the unconscious that is structured like a language but is heard like a Letter: we ought to be at least responsible to carry the burden of our own speech, and raise a voice- not too much of a silence: to raise a voice towards those teeth accountable for producing almighty discourses leading to cloning, that is, those phonemes crashing subjectivity within the cultural discourses denying the subjects' right to create their own place and their own alphabet- that place that is in- formation: Freud's staying in Austria until the outmost moment has something to teach regarding this heroic stance, an Act not worthy of an Actor but of an Activist· it is not a support or a submission to the death drive but to life.

Not to be Anarthrous: this is not the duty of the analyst as a person or as a position, but as a Kinesis: it is psychoanalysis own duty to whose ethic one's desire dedicates his being into the service of the Cause· we ought to think finer than the mass of the analytic room and further that the meters of the area covered by the signifier we assume we recognize- because they ought to recognize, those signifiers, one's desire instead because master signifiers are attracted to desire· for this duty there is no payment- psychoanalysis returns to civilization what it has borrowed· the analyst marks the discourses in various ways as to allow liberty for desire- subjects are holding the Letters of the word psychoanalyst because of their desire alone: that should have been enough to direct one's being and Act· the act is a response to a binary interpretation of the analysand- opposite of acting out· it is occurred with nauseating responsibility and the ability to carry the burden of one's act and speech: a new Aladdin could have wished from the jinni that analysts speak more and read less when presenting- it should have been the minimum received by their cephalic abilities from their formation, for, the Act demands an interpretation from the analysand- another threshold to be crossed· the trauma localizes· desire moves: it roars- I do not negotiate· and let it be.

That is a diorama for a School of the Letter.

On the Reading that is Symphonic.

The Act is the antiphony of jouissance- the phoneme ought to be sang and spelled out· a school and an orientation could have create a chorus, at least regarding the direction of a desire, and to the best of our stupidity we could have made some use of the Liturgia Horarum, for, if there is anything to be venerated, that is not the semblance but that desire for the Cause, not its causality, but that which becomes a breath from the puncture, for, the fissure from where desire shall sprang its motion is for no use but for Kinesis and for the Letter, not a waste of a litter certainly but an abysmal aether, offering the trauma's sacred pinches and tones to the analyst's desire· it is in this asymmetrical manner that the signifier detects and recognizes the analysts, not the other way around, and within this creation, not an existence, analysts are desired to learn a novel alphabet: each time de novo, for, and because every analysand is different, an analyst is dissimilar, as well, to its own shadow.

To that mysterious syllabary, the seesawed with the subdividing elements presented to desire, the so fundamentals of lyrical euphonies, as unfathomable compression of another Paraclete who offers its ParOusia with every manifestation of those Letters, analysts have faith too- the faith to the process and its motion, to which, as not predestined before hand, we ought to dedicate the being who desires to its musical chords· such a calligraphic voice out to doxologize, that the Ethic is not a rule but a bearing, away, definitely, from the twofold of good or evil, of deontological or axiological ethics: away from the normative and towards the feminization of the ethic itself.

Once a reading is based on the signifier not taking in consideration the feminine Letter, it cannot be an Act· the Sinthome is the reason for a Cause, not causing a reason out of it- let us, instead of living with, to die with the Sinthome- let us choose the demise to which a being admeasures its cause and lunacy- let us have the sense of hearing Freud: that should have been enough of a reason for a subject to Cause life· and that is causality.

The Holy Spirit: The Breath, which cannot be Said.

That Real, which cannot be said, is an Act- it is a Being Silent, for, that which cannot be said is a breath, the phoneme's, or, even better, the Letter's lungful of air · for, the clothes of the king were invisible and yet, the body, that audible membrane perceived as the product of the Other's Gaze- what a mistaken perception· and, if the practise of psychoanalysis, as much as that is formulated onto Freud's discovery and towards the sanctified direction for the cause initiated by Lacan, then, what a foolishness is to be, to investigate that which cannot be said of the Real by speaking about it, when, when my dear friend, you ought to know a better joke to a-muse us, through your own experience of that gap · that Real, which is restricted, is the hole overflowing with desire and, from where, a subject recites neither a prayer nor a speech- but a breath of cool heavenly breeze, and it preserves only the nomination of desire and its rite de passage, forcing a subject, a given one, to say This is where I should be, for, here I desire, therefore I breath: and, in the hunt for noble words, or at least a few amusing syllables, to be able to declare a, not many, words of honesty, and surely less of intellectualism, for something that is quite a new creation with each and for each subject, then, let us cough and scratch that which tickles our throat, and ingest our tongues' glossalgia, once again, out of pain and because there is, so far, inscrutability and continuation of faith to the mystery of the question, not what, but how is it to be a human being, not that which speaks of its desire but, that, that who also acts on it- it is with the act, dignified friend, that, that which cannot be said becomes a breath, one of desire: the Lectis Thing of the ErgOn.

Aristotle, as a philosopher, beamed his illuminated words, akin to a star not to descend, indeed he did, that Ousia is that which cannot be said: what can we say, as psychoanalysts, authorised with responsibility from Freud's discovery of the unconscious, about that which cannot be said- if not that it is an Act· and, have you been paying any attention to Lacan's seminar on the Act, in case the experience of psychoanalysis has not exposed you to this truth, not, of course, reducing its mystery into a final product worthy of a technical device, yet named as Lacanian, out of stinginess and the inability to share, even after two hundred years of psychoanalysis onto your tethered body, you would be able to grasp the references to the holy spirit, to that nomination of fire: it is that which cannot be said, because it is a tongue of inferno enabling another given analyst to learn an alphabet that he does not know· the psychoanalytic Act begins with xenoglosia: this is its Ethic and it could become a strong Zephyr of an anabatic wind, another sort of a breath, just to push and create some, as Bruno De Florence said, waves of desire· it is too boring to sit on the sand and enjoy the sun- when one's desire is the wind itself.

And, certainly and bravely enough, you can speak of your ethic- that is the Real of our practise, if we continue to Babel it, not label it, Freudian· for, the Hypostases of the Letters is not the Υποκείμενον but the 'Υποκείμενον Acting on its desire, an Act and Word having one Ousia: that is the true Parousia of desiring subjects and of any psychoanalytic formation · the Πρώτες Ουσίες, and God, are one- for Ον and God are mere Letters of that Ουσία, which is feminine: She is a Breath- she is not the Other but the Alien.

On the Faith of Psychoanalysts: A Cause of Desire, Which is a Cause.

The signifier is acrostic to the Letter's Ousia- not homoousian: it is the Summa Theologica of the Epistula Purloined: and it can be that, because the Act is autonomous, as much as the master signifiers designating the trauma and its destiny, wreathing, and not breathing, with all the musicality of its arias· that faith is indeed the praxis of the subject, an Alien Act to the binary of idolatry of the One and or the Other, not of the Agalma- certainly not that of Pygmalion, whose The Woman has been exteriorized through, and by, a marble stature, a procedure in opposition to that of Orpheus' and Lot's faith, with the subsequent man having his name signifying the veil in Hebrew, a veil he did not use because he subtracted his own faith· idolographical, that is a much better of a word for an epistolary poet who has not yet written, not yet, for, the principle is that of desire, a motion in itself and not bound in the ethics of philosophy as it is that which binds an ethic· and, if the Πίστις of the Greeks, with a small object cause of desire in its front, just a small letter α, so to turn the word α-πίστις, and terracing faith to the object cause, which is a cause, the analytic cause, in other words, that is an ethic in its own fundamental nature, then the trust and faith of the analyst is to have a good laugh with the still scientific melancholia of Russell, who, as a true fanatical obsessive seeking to erase any demand alluding to a desire, he commands the subject to bring to an end the process of a delicate science, by saying that, When there is evidence, no one speaks of faith: but dear Bertrand, it is those evidence that aggravate a spirit to request faith.

Devotion to a Cause, of desire, is the course of action itself where, and wherein, the subject agglomerates his intimate science· let us just declare of a whisper's lethargic libretto, dreamed up, one of those allegories where there is no animal but in its absence, an animal which is not only political but acting too, saying: I Act, therefore I Desire- this is the ErgOn· the doing is rational, the Act is faith and desires from, and towards, the cause· faith is a Cause: it is human· and, if the fundamental rule of free association, that which is to be crossed and viaducted as an indispensable threshold most wanted for the Act of psychoanalysis so the subject becomes an Act of its desire, could vandalize a verbalization of an acrostic alphabet, those Letters that the subject cores in and within the signifiers, that, indeed, that would have been a wild analysis to the ears of a commanding priest- when in fact it is a truth not, alas, schooling analysts: I Desire, therefore I Act: I Act, therefore, I do not speak, for I have faith to my duty.

It is enough of a word- that is an act- to say: this is how you should speak of the end of an analysis: when there is a beginning.

Free Association: On a Function to be Revised

Free associate your Breath, dear analyst, because, from the everything, that Apeiron, comes the pneuma but not through the Other's free concurrence - how much does an aristocrat enjoy listening to what he already knows yet behaving as if not acknowledging· for, he cannot listen if the, which it is, the breath, the object a, and the Letter are homoousian to the Das Ding, separated but not divided, not, not with the cut that enables signifiers to appear but with the ditinic comma, which is the spiritus asper of the Act, not the action, of breathing· the Dasia, or, the tones of Pythagoras, whom masters of psychoanalysis in their divine struggle with time and the unconscious speak of musicality- how can the ear of he who has no faith and has never conducted a poem in favor of the muses can have a word about music, he that cannot speak a word deriving from his own poetry· and, to these unfaithful who research knowledge, belief and faith, that is, to those who have never experienced the vomiting breath of a fricative consonant, neither the kindness of the Spiritus Lenis, that horizontal breathing which the Greeks have submitted as high spirit, the Ψιλόν Πνεύμα, marking the nonattendance of the right to be heard, not to be or respire because the letter's flux has been eternalized by the signifier: it is this function upon the breathing letters, the subtraction of the signifier's oxygen, wrongfully taken for litter as the hypokeimenon, the subject of the unconscious, cannot subsist without the Ousia.

And, if you force air out of your lungs, that is unquestionably not a breath, but a doing of a poisoned breathing, an action and not an Act, for, that mouthful of air is produced by the two Lord articulators to whose reign desire supposed to pass through· and, if absolute difference is the desire of the analyst, that testimony has been so far an immense gaffe, since, walking the path that the Other does not exist, filing the subject's space with the truly heavy signature of responsibility, the practice ought to plead guilty even without a murky hand on a poor man's Bible, that the one-by-one, which is an Act, an Act not representing itself for one another as does the signifier, then, the everyone, every-one, is a subtraction referring to the accountability of the each· and, to that Evangelist's writings and speeches, he who is truly worthy, if the times would have allowed that, to be part of the church of Antioch, that speaks of Lacan as a technical device and not as an Ousia that is a seed to be thrown within good soil, but as a high-quality seed engineered to penetrate the soil which is what the discourse of the master leads them to· hence, to him, and also to that representing the silly deeds of Antioch, that the analyst is free associated as a creation, not from nothing but from Apeiron, for, the Ousia of psychoanalysis, in reference to transmission, is the desire but not without ParOusia, in close relation to transmission and the current and future generation of analysts· it is that Ousia, that which cannot be separated and a function to be revised from Parousia, this presence of desire.

Not for absolute difference, in terms of the Other or of the Same, because this algebra implies the presence of the Other to whom and which the subject is to be differentiated from by generating anew its breath: the each one, the presence and the dissimilar, is the Alien that cannot be a semblance to an image that does not exist and is diaphanous to its own vision: and that requires a formation to be created, not ex nihilo but ex Ousia: it requires poetry, and, even though and even through, the pitiful devil of phonetics scans and bears the weight of a witness that ex Ousia sounds akin to Εξουσία, which is ruling, then, we ought to spit a few phonemes, clear ones from the decomposed inhalation of a emit that has been tasting human soft tissue, by saying that ex Ousia is the desire functioning as a compass, those Ethics, and the essence which allows for the flux of transmission for rediscovery and re-nomination: and if we want to discuss the disgusted dialogue with that Other whom enjoys Anousia, be that of desire, that is to have a word in terms of authority- what can we say more than that the analyst places his whole being within that which desires: not, hopefully not, a psychoanalysis that is Ex Opere Operato· one by one to be free associated· and, if there is an incredible something we ought to be qualified is to forget the mother tongue's implementation as a humidity-burdened ambiance, to which a fake breathing is not dramatically glowing since it hides its responsibility behind the master: this is the destiny of the proverb's architect, where one creates and the idiot repeats- that comes in plural: that function is to Seeing its own Breathing, not to see· but, that, demands very terrible language rules because desire rests within a diphthong and not a holophrase· I can already hear analysts counting the number of the letters in an alphabet: a good revision to start with.

On the Breath of the Das Ding

And, from the hither, that here cognominated by those libidinous syllables and letters spelling the analysand's Apraxia, that, that which traps the analyst in his own disposition unable to animate the eupnea's formation, a breath that desires and the pulsating heart of the Das Ding, which is a breath, a letter and the allelomorphic cough of the cause's representative, that is, that which causes desire, analysts are decomposed by accumulating freely the alphabet· and yet, and hopefully then, the parallelogramic equation of the analyst's kinesis within this Act functioning as a plasma, a matter equipoising a mystery of ensarkosis without a first cause, can have some intimate thoughts about, not poetry alone but Allopoiesis, since, and along these unfathomable vernaculars, a systematic phenomenology of the Other becomes Alien because the system produces an account different from the system itself· and when then Gentile, he who becomes more feminine in spelling and less masculine in the system of the signifier's gnosis within the structure of the Other and enters time itself with precision, because, as an object cause it moves in the vicinity of the arrow supposed to strike it, and carries into the open a blaspheme to the ears of the messengers who have become agronomists of the bad seed, the desire in the dream seeks instead of the analyst seeking the symbol: for that, the direction of a formation is from the Logos to the Myth because sexual relationship cannot do without it, without that magical realism to whom Herodotus has been more faithful than Thucydides- a myth of xenoglossy for him, that analyst, who is afraid to encounter the infamous vagina dentate because he still holds his practice from his penis: it is he, who produces the blastheme because he is not causing any agrammatism to Lacan's own signifiers, but becomes a true teacher- a Pythia who interprets by herself: that is a vagina dentate, without a doubt.

There is too much composure and synchronization in this harvest and a fruit that certainly looks beautiful- that is what is worrying because desire moves with worms and prostitutes· mouths are silenced on their own choice, as if to produce an allegory of not disturbing the immaculate monster, one that they have placed onto the throne so to attempt to steal or to be given an advance on behalf of the gnosis of the invented secrecy of the singifier· and, for the not payment, that road not leading but is guided by the ethos that wishes, the system outgrowths sleeping actors and not activists valuable for a paralysis and not analysis, because those tonques have been dipped into the honey of mimicry and impersonation of a certain Alexia, a Semiosis from which their own lexis is absent- and if they do not have a righteous tome to which they have faith to, one just to keep at bay the theory of their own irresponsibility, they turn their attention to the Etymologicum Magnum of psychoanalysis· it is inconceivable to the Sadducees that the reading, or, better, the spelling of the ethics' superparticular ratio, be that with the monochord psalmodicon, those four fundamental concepts serving as the tetractys, deliberates from and on a monochord beyond the subject supposed to know· and that the Βίος of Heraclitus is not, not a bow but an organ for the Kinesis of the Letter, exactly akin to the psalmodicon: from above the streams flow and mark and yet it is ID itself that is marked by that everything, for, the best way up is the way down and from the river to the firmament: and, how could it be to bathe one's gaze in its waters: behold, the breath of the Das Ding· a poet ought to ask Dante how did he administer the tuning of his breathing with the bouquet of death: that is how the Letter is seen- as a river. And, if the Hypokeimenon's breath is not containing the fore-boding of the object cause and of the letter's kinesis, then, the

Breath's metousiosis births Lamella itself.· not from above but from within: the Act is a Real Presence, a Parousia.

On the Ousia that is Feminine but not of a Woman

And, from the lo and behold of a proposition which is not the result of a psaltery's pseudepigraphic composition within and beyond the threshold of the Act demanding not of the wisdom of Solomon but of the reception of *"The key to the world in the split of the prepubescent, the psychoanalyst no longer has to expect a look, but sees himself become a voice·"* and from that Voice, powders the first Ανάγκη and yet not in particles· and, that is not discourse- it is a breath and a letter, unparticular and not in particles, from which the discourse and the Voice mark the lamina of destiny and time upon the subject and its flesh to embody the word and the signifier· those are Homoousian to the Das Ding, the Letters, the Breath and that which causes desire but itself cannot desire unless privated and ex-posed at the same time to the gnosis of holiness and carnal acquaintances for that which is sup-positional to prevail in immaculation, not emasculation, and, from whose kernel shall a homo-ousia that is not a man, produce the digammon Stigma to become the episemon six within the signifier, for the letter becomes a number, and from the mark is fashioned sex: this is a riddle· for, the question to mark the tantalized nerves of a psychoanalyst's transference to the Cause is, not what is a woman, or, what does she want, but, what is not a man: what does not have a phallus but is not a woman, and not an object with No-Body, a being which, in its silence, even among the spectrum of the perversion of perversions, one cannot copulate with and breed devils· to this, the various generations of analysts ought to give us a testimony.

The signifier is the result of the letter's misshaped schema because of an apogeetic circumgyration dazed to admire the supposed meaning, no, not of the Not-all but of the All-knots, to which, often with the gaze, never with the voice, a number is the logical and not the diphthong: thus the cut elaborates the signifier and not the letter, dear friend, for, to caress the γράμμα with an intervention you ought to read the theophoric names, τετραγράμματον, and that, for the inspiration of your spirited desire, can only happen with a crafted hymn devoted to the practice of de-masculation but not feminization· and because in the beginning of an analysis the analyst is presented with a farce, and because analysts ought to laugh with a simpleton's knowledge of peasantry that is theirs, as another subject who supposed to laugh because it has experienced the joke, one more comical than dramatically structured in the Real of the clinic, when the threshold is passed, assumed that, at first, one obtains the allegory by which Ali Baba uses the letters in the abracadabra of the nameable Open Sesame- there is the Ousia, which is beyond the Other and towards the Alien· it is here that we could mumble the *Allopoiesis*.

But do not be fooled from the Άλλος meaning the Other: autopoiesis is not poetry and surely not the sinthome· allopoiesis, although derived from the same Ousia let us say, the ParOusia has nothing in common to the inquiry of What had initiated it: it is even more furthered that this, or poles apart from the absolute difference of a desire that needs the Other to which it shall be the difference- a hysterical desire but not feminine· hence, next to the auxiliary of this threshold's comedy and to that key's proposition, there is no principle or structure to which the Ergon that is of the Letter, not the subject that is of the signifier, functions as an absolute different from· and, yet again, let us mention between thieves the ParOusia and have an orientation to the secrecy of a communion of a being who acts of its word: although the concept of Real Presence is interpreted variously by the denominations, we shall prefer the witticism sleeping as a beauty between the gap of the I know nothing and the It is a mystery, just to grasp the attendance of the Real Presence of the human enigma, and the absence or dissolution of fantasy that comes with the structure, the Other, the Signifier in terms of the Ousia· the first Ανάγκη for analysts is the Breath of the Letters and not the Discourse, which demands their flux, union or stasis to have a saying, be that meaningless· the signifier is the Abecedarium Stasis: and if the Chinese do not have a use for psychoanalysis, it is because they can breathe their letters, for, in the beginning it was the deed, that of the letter punctuating the breath: in the beginning there is the Act, this Breath of the One-all-Alone, without the Other· in the beginning, it is the letter, not was: Before Abraham, I Am- and this is a joke of some import to investigate with a laughter, as far as we are concerned with the flux of Ousia.